KENT CRICKETING GREATS

MARK BENSON

Kent
Cricketing Greats

53 of the best cricketers for Kent, 1869-1989

by Dean Hayes

Foreword by Colin Cowdrey CBE

SPELLMOUNT LTD
TUNBRIDGE WELLS, KENT

First published in the UK in 1990 by
SPELLMOUNT LTD
12 Dene Way, Speldhurst
Tunbridge Wells, Kent TN3 0NX

British Library Cataloguing in Publication Data
Hayes, Dean P, 1949-
  Kent cricketing greats. – (County cricketing greats).
  1. Kent. County cricket. Clubs. Kent County Cricket
    Club.
  Biographies. Collections
  I. Title   II. Series
  796.3580922

ISBN 0-946771-74-X

Design by Projects Thirty-Seven, Paddock Wood
Printed in Great Britain by
Biddles Ltd, Guildford, Surrey

Acknowledgements

I am greatly indebted to the following for their help in the compilation of this book: E W Swanton, Chris Taylor, Peter Foster and Colin Cowdrey who has kindly who has kindly written the foreword.

Further thanks to Peter A Stafford (ex-Bolton League Secretary) whose cricket library is second to none!

The illustrations and statistics were kindly provided by Chris Taylor (Archivist of Kent County Cricket Club). The picture of C I Thornton was supplied by David Frith of *Wisden Cricket Monthly*.

In the Spellmount/Nutshell Cricket list:

Contents

Foreword

To have played on the St Lawrence Ground under a Kent captain is a huge honour. There is nothing like Kentish pride, nor anything to match the atmosphere or happy sense of occasion in Canterbury week.

He is a dull cricketer who has played at Canterbury oblivious to the ghosts of the great players and their deeds on the same lovely sward, the scene little altered over the hundred years.

Under Lord Harris' autocratic but kindly hand, J R Mason, superb cricketer, led a fine side to our first County Championship title in 1906.

We can picture them all thanks to the glorious Chevalier Taylor painting which hangs proudly in the Pavilion.

Colin Blythe bowls from the Pavilion End, Huish behind the stumps, J R Mason at slip, lithe and tall brilliant out fielder K L Hutchings, fast bowler Arthur Fielder, Humphreys, Dillon, Findlay, Blaker, Marsham, Burnup, Seymour, heroes all – what a side.

Twenty-five years later, Tich Freeman took root at that same Pavilion End, wheeling away his leg spinners with Leslie Ames keeping wicket, quiet and gentle executioner with the gloves. Freeman was to take more than a thousand wickets in four years. But Leslie Ames, the batsman, changed character as he launched himself at every type of bowler, scoring a hundred hundreds, only one of them in more than three hours.

Yet Kent boasted so many high quality attacking batsmen. Bill Ashdown, Percy Chapman and Bryan Valentine supreme, but none to match the genius of Frank Woolley, as good an allrounder that has ever graced the game. His commanding presence at the crease acted as a magnet to the villagers of Kent winding their way through the country lanes for a glimpse of his mastery and a memory to take away with them to feast on for life. It was freakish that Godfrey Evans should emerge as a more billiant wicket keeper than his mentor, Leslie Ames, and that he should be followed by a genius in Alan Knott.

If Ames feasted upon Tich Freeman, Godfrey Evans formed a marvellous combination with Douglas Wright, one of the greatest attacking leg spin and googly bowlers of all time. Then, Alan Knott will always be associated with the inimitable Derek Underwood.

Mike Denness and Brian Luckhurst formed a fine opening partnership, the equal of Fagg and Todd. There came two brilliant cricketers from overseas, John Shepherd and Asif Iqbal and they made a rich contribution to the Kent scene, making friends wherever they went.

It was my good luck to be Captain, with Leslie Ames at my side as Manager, as Kent's fortunes rallied again and we won the Championship in 1970, the first time for 57 years.

How often over a twenty-five year career I allowed my mind to wander in the field and day dream and picture the greats of Kent – and this lovely book captures the feats of fifty-three of them.

Dedication

To my Mother

Introduction

The history of Kent cricket is almost as old as the game itself. The earliest reference of all relating to the county mentions 'cricketing' between Weald and Upland near Chevening in 1610. The game was spreading quickly through Kent and was among the 'vain and sinful customes of sports' which were played on Sundays at Maidstone before 1635. We also hear of a match at Coxheath in 1646, but the most celebrated seventeenth century reference to Kent cricket comes from the rate book of the Church of St John the Baptist, Eltham, in 1654, during the Commonwealth period. This book recorded the occasion when the church-wardens and overseers decided to fine seven parishioners for being cricket players on 'ye Lord's day'.

The Commonwealth period was very important for the development of cricket. The Royalist gentry had to retreat to their country estates for amusement. So from then on the Wealden gentlemen were the Patrons of the game. Among the most notable of the aristocratic patrons of Kent cricket, were the Sackvilles of Knole and the Sidneys of Penshurst.

In 1728 we hear of a match at Penshurst between Kent, led by Edwin Stead of Harrietsham, and Sussex, led by Sir William Gage. The match was played for fifty guineas and we learn that for 'the third time this summer, the Kent men have been too expert for those of Sussex'. In 1729 Kent played a combined team from the three counties of Hampshire, Surrey and Sussex.

The leader in these Kent enterprises was Edwin Stead, who died in 1735. After his death, Kent were forced to look for fresh leadership; it came in the form of the Second Duke of Dorset and his brother Lord John Sackville. It was he who opened for Kent in the celebrated match against All England at the Artillery Ground, London on 18 June 1744

Not so long after this match the Hambledon Club came into prominence, but Kent had a batsman who was greatly feared by the Hambledon bowlers, his name was Joseph Miller. Another of Kent's great patrons in the second half of the eighteenth century was Sir Horatio Mann, who appropriately enough, was born in 1744, on the day of the Kent v All England match. Of twenty-seven matches recorded between 1768 and 1787 between Kent and Hambledon, Kent won twelve and lost thirteen – one match was drawn and one match tied.

The leading Kent players in the early 1800s were John Willes and Herbert Jenner. Willes went down in cricket history as the man who stormed out of Lord's whilst playing for a Kent XI against the MCC. He had been no-balled for his round-arm action. Herber Jenner (later Jenner-Fust and MCC President) had been largely responsible for the first Varsity Match in 1827.

A golden age for Kent cricket occurred between the years 1834 and 1850. The county produced a side that was worthy to rank alongside any other county side of any time. In fact, it was a side that for years often defeated England. Kent had five great players, they have been immortalised in the lines:

> And with five such mighty cricketers, t'was but natural to win,
> As Felix, Wenman, Hillyer, Fuller Pitch and Alfred Mynn.

Mynn was the 'Lion of Kent'. He was about six foot one inch and weighed around eighteen stone. He was the most destructive fast bowler in England. One of his deliveries caused a fielder at long-stop to spit blood for a fortnight after the ball had struck him in the chest! He was also a dangerous batsman and a fine slip-fielder; he was one of the best loved of all Kent cricketers.

Felix, whose real name was Nicholas Wanostracht, was a superb left-handed batsman. He was a man of many talents – he invented a bowling machine and 'tubular' cricket gloves. Edward Wenman was the leading wicket-keeper in England. He would often stand up to the bowling of Alfred Mynn and was skilful on the leg-side. Wenman was also a good batsman and the much respected captain of the side. William Hillyer was the most effective medium-pace bowler of the day. Fuller Pitch, originally from Norfolk, was probably the best batsman who had played cricket up to that time. Also, as in any other great side, there were plenty of other good players in support.

The effect of all these players on Kent cricket was at once apparent. Between 1835 and 1849, Kent played thirty-one games against England, winning seventeen of them. This successful side broke up around 1860, thereafter, they lost eight out of the next ten of these fixtures.

The only top class professional for Kent in the next two decades was Edgar Willisher. He was a fast left-handed bowler, who had much to do with the legalising of overarm bowling. Willisher in fact, links the Kent side of Mynn and Pitch with that of Lord Harris, so long was his playing career.

There were, at this time, two rival clubs: one centred on Canterbury, the other on Maidstone. This clearly wasn't good for Kent cricket as a whole. Wisden tells us that in 1865, the Maidstone club passed a resolution that 'The cricket of the County might be much improved if an amalgmation of this club with the club at Canterbury could be arranged without interfering with the maintenance of the Canterbury Grand Cricket Week in its integrity.'

Nothing happened immediately, but on 22 October 1870 a meeting was held at the Royal Fountain Hotel, Canterbury. The most important resolution was the first: 'That the Kent County Cricket Club and the Beverley Kent Cricket Club be amalgamated in one Club, to be called the

Kent County Cricket Club; and that Canterbury be the head-quarters of the Club. Matches to be played on grounds to be named by the Committee.' This was passed and so one hundred and twenty years ago Kent County Cricket Club, as we know it today, was born.

The year of 1875 was a turning point in Kent's history. This was the year that Lord Harris became Captain, Honorary Secretary and President of Kent all in one go! He was a formidable, but fair, man and a strong leader. He remained a Trustee of Kent until his death in 1932. He was captain for fifteen seasons and held the position of secretary until 1880. One of his greatest achievements was in rescuing the Band of Brothers from oblivion in the mid-1870s. The club had been founded in 1858 and had declined rapidly, but under Lord Harris it soon began to flourish. Lord Harris was also a batsman of genuine class and was able to persuade the better amateurs of the day, of whom Kent always had sufficient, to play county cricket instead of country-house cricket.

The greatest achievement of Kent in this period was to beat the Australians five times in fifteen years. In 1884, when Kent assembled their best side, they were the only county team to beat the Australian touring team. Among the players of this time were Frank Penn, a fine batsman, whose career was unfortunately shortened by ill-health; Stanley Christopherson, a fast-bowler and later President of the MCC who broke down in 1886; the brothers Alec and George Hearne both good all-rounders; E F S Tylecote, one of the best wicket-keeper batsmen of the day and 'Nutty' Martin who had figures of 12 for 102 in his only Australian Test.

By 1897 the Kent Nursery, which functioned on the Angel Ground at Tonbridge, had been established. It was the most important decision in the story of Kent's cricket. It was the foundation of the team's success, the Nursery being a testament to the coaching skills of Captain William McCanlis. McCanlis himself had been a fairly modest county player with Kent in the 1860s and 1870s. However, he proved that he had the talent of passing on the technicalities of the game on one hand and an enthusiasm for the game on the other. From now on there was a supply of good professionals to supplement the amateurs. In fact, no fewer than eighteen players attending the Tonbridge Nursery after 1897 went on to gain county caps, twelve of them for Kent.

Kent were no longer dependent on getting the best amateurs into the field together. In 1906, when Kent won the County Championship for the first time, their side contained either five or all six of the following: Colin Blythe, Arthur Fielder and Frank Woolley, all famous Test cricketers and Bill Fairservice, 'Punter' Humphreys and Jim Seymour, all of whom made valuable contributions. There is, perhaps, no other side that one would have wished to have seen. Leng's Cricket Handbook of the following year said that Kent's victory was 'extraordinarily popular, a result due to the brilliant character of their play and their splendid sportsmanship.'

The outstanding bowler in that 1906 season was the quick and dangerous right-arm bowler, Arthur Fielder, superbly aided behind the wicket by Fred Huish. Colin Blythe was at his peak as a slow left-arm bowler and Kenneth Hutchings, for two months, was being rated as one of the most dangerous batsmen in England. Wisden in fact described him as 'the English Trumper', the 'sensation of the 1906 season'. There was also the arrival of a young colt by the name of Frank Woolley – however, in 1906 he had to contest the one vacancy with both Fairservice and Humphreys. C J Burnup hadn't played for almost two seasons, but he returned to bat superbly, heading the averages with 69.75. In the Canterbury Week that season, Kent scored 568 against Sussex and 479 against Lancashire – winning both games by an innings. The match at Bournemouth against Hampshire was the one to decide the Championship. Kent had to avoid defeat; the young colt, Woolley, was sent in first as Kent batting second amassed 610 in just six hours. Even so, in the last week of August it seemed mathematically impossible for Kent to win the Championship unless Yorkshire were beaten. However, thanks to some shrewd bowling by Gilbert Jessop, Gloucestershire beat Yorkshire by one run and the County Championship was Kent's.

The next Championship successes in 1909 and 1910 were aided by the bowling of Blythe and Woolley on slow pitches that often made them unplayable. Colin Blythe in 1909 took 215 wickets, the year that E W Dillon took over the Kent captaincy. In 1910 Kent had won the County Championship by 12 August. During those two seasons Kent had the successful opening pair of Hardinge and Humphreys, followed by Seymour, Woolley and Hubble – quite a formidable batting line-up. In 1909 a 37-year-old by the name of D W Carr emerged as a bowler of googlies and leg-breaks and was immediately capped by England, even before he'd played at county level! Another player who made an important contribution was Bill Bradley, a formidable fast bowler.

In 1913 Kent won the County Championship for the fourth time. In 1908 and 1911 the county were runners-up – it was an outstanding period in the County's history.

In Kent's four oustanding seasons, their results were:

	Played	Won	Drawn	Lost
1906	22	16	4	2
1909	26	16	8	2
1910	25	19	3	3
1913	28	20	5	3

Six men: Blythe, Fairservice, Fielder, Humphreys, Huish and Seymour, were regular members of the eleven in all four Championship years and Dillon, Hutchings, Mason and Woolley played in three of them.

After the First World War, Kent usually remained near the top of the Championship Table, but they didn't sustain their outstanding form of the pre-war period and never won a title between the wars. Two men dominated Kent cricket in this period, Frank Woolley and 'Tich' Freeman.

Frank Woolley was probably the most famous Kent player of modern times. He was a genuine all-rounder. His batting was graceful and effective; every year after the war, until he retired at the end of the 1938 season, he scored well over 1,000 runs. He scored 2,000 runs or more on eleven occasions and in 1928 he hit 3,352 runs, including twelve centuries. Altogether for Kent in first-class matches, he scored 47,868 runs. For years, he was one of the best slow left-hand bowlers in the world, filling the void left by Colin Blythe. His best year with the ball was 1920, when he took 185 wickets. In first-class matches he claimed 1,680 wickets. At the same time he was picking up catches at slip, taking more than anyone in the game except the wicket-keeper, 1,018! taker

'Tich' Freeman was the greatest wicket-keeper taker any county has ever had. He had a great command of top spin and googly, this along with his exceptional accuracy made him the most feared leg-spinner in the game. He was greatly aided by Les Ames behind the wicket and Woolley at slip, regularly taking more than 200 wickets a season. Freeman's most productive season was 1928, when he took 304 wickets. In all matches he took 3,776 wickets at an averyage of only 18 runs each. He was, there is no doubt, a brilliant bowler, but these figures go to show how different county cricket was in the days when most counties had at least one leg-spinner in the side.

It was unfortunate for Kent that 'Tich' Freeman didn't have the support of another front-line bowler in the 1920s and 1930s. However, C S Marriott was available in the school holidays to bowl his faster leg-breaks. In fact, it has been said that when Freeman and Marriott were both on form and bowling together, many batsmen preferred to face 'Tich'! Another great, although a different type of leg-spinner, made his Kent debut in 1932, his name Doug Wright.

Kent's batting between the wars was never much of a problem. The most notable amateur batsman of the day was Percy Chapman. He could take any attack in the country apart. After good performances for Cambridge and The Gentlemen, he was made captain of England in 1926 for the match at the Oval. The following season, when Kent entertained Lancashire at Maidstone, Chapman made 260 in just three hours. Kent had been reduced to 70 for 5, when Chapman proceeded to murder the Red-Rose bowling and Ted McDonald in particular. Chapman was also a great fielder and inspirational captain. Jack Hubble had retired and his successor, Les Ames, was by a long way the greatest wicket-keeper batsman in the country. Chapman's predecessors included Lionel

Troughton who was also captain before the war; his successors, Bryan Valentine and Gerry Chalk. Bryan Valentine was an outstanding batsman, one of many brilliant Kent amateurs, who included J L Bryan, A M Crawley, J G W Davies and C H Knott. Kent also had the services of three long-serving professionals, Bill Ashdown, Arthur Fagg and Leslie Todd, all of whom made valuable and consistent performances. These players by no means exhaust the list and so the question must be asked: why Kent were not the Champions? The probable answer seems to be that they threw too many matches away to achieve the consistency needed to win the Championship.

After a bright start following the Second World War, the county fell on hard times. It still possessed outstanding players of individual character. Perhaps the greatest was Doug Wright, often brilliant and very unpredictable. He was a leg-spinner of unusual quality, possessing speed, bounce and great spin. Fred Ridgway proved himself to be a reliable pace-bowler, possessing great stamina. Another opening bowler to impress in the first couple of decades since the war was Dave Halfyard. Behind the wickets was the most brilliant, if not the most consistent of all England wicket-keepers, Godfrey Evans. As a batting side, Kent had the experienced Les Ames (who had retired from behind the stumps and continued purely as a batsman) and the three stalwarts from pre-war, Valentine, Fagg and Todd. In 1950, a 17-year-old Tonbridge schoolboy made his debut for Kent, his name, Colin Cowdrey. His career spanned such a period, that he faced Lindwall and Miller and then Lillee and Thomson! The Kent line-up was augmented by other players who were to provide loyal service; these included Alan Dixon, Arthur Phebey, Bob Wilson, Stuart Leary, and Colin Page who became the County's manager, succeeding Les Ames.

As one might imagine from this impressive list of players, Kent were a very interesting side to watch, but unfortunately they were none too successful.

In 1964 Kent finished seventh in the County Championship and this improvement continued over the next few years until, in 1970, they won the Championship. In fact, in the eleven seasons between 1967 and 1977, Kent won eleven trophies. In 1967, Kent won the Gillette Cup and finished as runners-up to Yorkshire in the County Championship. The following season saw Kent finish again in second spot in the Championship.

In 1970 Kent celebrated their centenary year by taking the County Championship title for the first time since 1913. They won it, despite losing most of their leading players at various stages of the season. Colin Cowdrey (captain), Mike Denness, Alan Knott, Brian Luckhurst and Derek Underwood all representing England. The winning of the Championship was all the more remarkable, Kent having been bottom of the table in July. In 1971 Kent won the Fenner Trophy, this signalling the end of Cowdrey's reign as captain. Another England captain, Mike Denness skippered Kent from 1972 to 1976. During his reign, Kent won the John Player League on three occasions, 1972, 1973 and 1976; the Benson and Heges Cup twice, 1973 and 1976; the Gillette Cup in 1974 and the Fenner Trophy in 1973. Asif Iqbal, a brilliant batsman and fielder from Pakistan was captain in 1977 when Kent shared the Schweppes Championship with Middlesex. The following year, Alan Ealham, a brilliant fielder anywhere and forcing batsman, took over the captaincy, leading Kent to the County Championship title and Benson and Hedges Cup.

As many people will rightly point out, this turn of fortune coincided with the start of special registration.

Kent bought very wisely! The magnificent Asif Iqbal and John Shepherd plus, for a shorter time, Bernard Julien, proved to be great assets.

Earlier in the years of success, Kent had the superb Cowdrey and two other international-class batsmen in Denness and Luckhurst. The former was a stylish batsman, the latter a rather more doughty competitor but, as an opening pair, they were very reliable. There were other stalwarts in the Kent side of these successful years: Graham Johnson, a fine all-round cricketer; Paul Downton, a wicket-keeper batsman who moved to Middlesex in 1980; Bob Woolmer, a batsman and medium-pace bowler who was invaluable to the county; and Alan Ealham the most modest of men. However, the most important contributions came from Derek Underwood. As early as 1963 he completed 100 wickets in his first season. Kent were the sole beneficiary of his unique bowling style which, but for World Series Cricket, would most certainly have made him the highest wicket-taker in Tests. His main accomplice was Alan Knott, a brilliant wicket-keeper batsman, who like 'Deadly' Underwood would have created more Test records if he hadn't played World Series Cricket in Australia.

In 1980 Kent fell away, but good young players were coming along, notably Mark Benson, Graham Dilley, Richard Ellison, Chris Tavare, and Chris Cowdrey who became Kent captain in 1985. In 1988 Kent were within one point of winning the County Championship, but it wasn't to be. Recently Alan Ealham has been restored to the fold, hoping eventually to become Kent's director of coaching.

Every county hopes the years ahead are bright and Kent are no exception. If I were writing this book in a few years' time, then players such as Graham Cowdrey, Alan Igglesden and Chris Penn would undoubtedly be included.

Kent are, in some ways, the most glamorous of county teams; they play on some very attractive grounds and have some remarkable feats of scoring to their credit.

They have also had some remarkable players, many of whom are celebrated in this book.

Les Ames

Birthplace:	Elham, Kent
Born:	3 December 1905
Died:	26 February 1990
Played:	1926-1951

Averages in all first-class Kent matches:

Matches	Innings	Not Outs	Runs	Highest Score	Average	100s
430	717	64	29,851	295	44.33	78

Runs	Wickets	Average	Best Analysis	5wI	10wM	Caught	Stumped
697	22	31.68	3 for 23	—	—	512	330

Number of Test Appearances: 47

Les Ames was born at Elham on 3 December 1905 and was associated with Kent cricket for sixty-six years, having first played for the Club and Ground and Second XI in 1924.

He entered big time cricket in the usual way, via school and his local club. By the time he was 14, he was successful as a batsman, playing for Harvey Grammar School, Folkestone, but wasn't given much chance to progress with his village side. He decided to move to Smeeth, now known as Mersham Hatch, where he soon made his mark. He moved on to Ashford and then to the Club and Ground and Kent Second XI.

He had never received any coaching as a wicket-keeper and to his surprise was asked to keep wicket in his first match for Kent Club and Ground at Hythe. In that match he claimed four victims: two caught and two stumped. The following summer he replaced the regular Kent Second XI keeper, Arthur Povey.

After playing twice for the county in 1926 he replaced Jack Hubble as wicket-keeper in 1927. In that season he passed a thousand runs for the first time, scoring 1,193 (average 35.08).

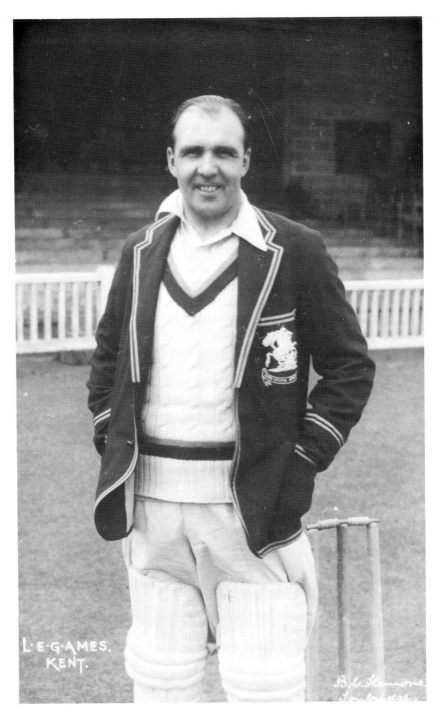

L·E·G·AMES.
KENT.

In 1928, Ames topped the thousand-run mark again, scoring 1,736 runs at an average of 36.16. His top score was 200, scored against Surrey at Blackheath. He helped to dismiss 121 batsmen that season (69 caught, 52 stumped), 114 of them coming in the County Championship. In the match against Oxford University at Fenners he claimed nine victims (8 caught, 1 stumped).

The following season saw Ames set a wicket-keeping record which has stood unchallenged since and which will never be approached unless the organisation of first-class cricket is once again radically altered. He dismissed 127 batsmen (79 caught, 48 stumped). His best peformance was in the match against Sussex at Maidstone, when he helped to dismiss 9 batsmen (5 caught, 4 stumped). He was selected as one of Wisden's Five Cricketers of the Year in 1929 with the words: 'Ames has a pretty style as a batsman and is not afraid to hit the ball full and hit it hard and he may become the best wicket-keeper batsman that England has ever had.' Ames also made his Test debut that summer at the Oval in the match against South Africa.

During 1929-30, he toured the West Indies, where the pace of the wickets suited him. He hit two hundreds on the tour, including his highest Test score of 149, made at Kingston. Altogether in the series, Ames scored 417 runs at an average of 59.57.

In 1930 he dismissed 85 batsmen (44 caught, 41 stumped), including 6 in one innings against Sussex at Folkestone.

In 1931 he was involved in two important batting partnerships; on both occasions the opponents were New Zealand. At Canterbury he and Frank Woolley put on 277 for the fifth wicket, still a Kent record. He and Gubby Allen put on 246 for the eighth wicket at Lord's.

Leslie Ames topped 2,000 runs the following season, scoring 2,100 runs at an average of 61.76. He scored three centuries in successive innings, 130 not out v Middlesex, 149 v Northamptonshire, and 120 v Surrey. Not a bad haul, if you bear in mind that a wicket-keeper's job by itself demands that he must watch every ball bowled, watch it bowled, how it is played, where it goes and how it is returned – this he must have done superbly, for to back up his runs he claimed 91 victims (35 caught, 56 stumped).

In 1933 Ames scored 3,058 runs in all first-class matches at an average of 58.80. He scored two double hundreds that summer, the first being 210 against Warwickshire at Tonbridge. Later he hit the highest score of his career, 295 against Gloucestershire at Folkestone. By nature he was a very attacking player and this innings took him only three-and-a-half hours. Twice before the war Ames won the Lawrence Trophy for the quickest hundred of the season, the years being 1936 and 1938. Also in that season of 1933 he hit hundreds in both innings in the match against Northamptonshire at Dover, 132 and 145 not out.

The following year saw him score 1,559 runs at an average of 57.74, his top score being 202 made against Essex in the match at Brentwood. However, his greatest innings was at Lord's that summer. When he joined Maurice Leyland, the Australians had England struggling somewhat at 182 for 5. Together they added 129, Leyand going for 109, Ames making 120. Verity, on a Lord's wicket ruined by rain, took 15 for 104 and England won by an innings, but without Ames's contribution the result could have been so different.

In 1935, during the Oval Test against South Africa, Ames scored the most runs ever made before lunch in a Test, 123. He started the morning on 25 not out, proceeding to 148 in magnificent fashion. After this season, a weak back made him ration his wicket-keeping and after 1938 he had to give it up altogether.

In 1937 he scored 1,997 runs (average 53.97) his top score being an unbeaten 201 against Warwickshire at Gillingham. He once again hit three centuries in successive innings: 125 v Worcestershire and then 119 and 127 in the same match against Surrey at Blackheath.

In his 47 Test matches, Ames scored eight centuries. One of these, 115, was made in 1938-39 against South Africa, when he shared a 197-run partnership with Wally Hammond. It remains the fourth wicket record between the two countries. His record as a batsman in Tests shows that he must have been a strong candidate for a place, even if he had never kept wicket. He scored 2,434 runs in Tests at an average of 40.56.

After the war Ames was batting just as well as he had been some six years earlier. After topping a thousand runs in 1946, he scored 2,156 runs in 1947 at an average of 67.37. His top score that season was an unbeaten 212 against Nottingham at Gravesend. He had another highly successful season in 1948, scoring 1,943 runs (average 45.18), his highest score being 212 against Gloucestershire at Dover.

In 1949 Les topped 2,000 runs, scoring 2,125 at an average of 47.22. He was the senior professional and many Kent followers were mystified when, that year, he was not appointed captain when Kent were looking for a successor to Bryan Valentine who had retired. Les states in *Kent – the winning eleven* that he was approached, but would have had to become an amateur. That didn't interest him, so he had no option but to decline the offer.

In 1950 Ames scored 1,347 runs at an average of 39.61. In the match at Bristol against Gloucestershire, he hit hundreds in both innings, 112 and 119. It was the third time he had achieved this feat. It was also the season when Ames scored his hundredth century. It came at Canterbury in the match against Middlesex. Kent had been set 237 to win in two-and-a-half hours. John Warr, the Middlesex pace-man, was repeatedly hit back over his head as Ames went down the wicket to him. Kent achieved victory with only a few minutes to spare. Ames's contribution was 131 out of 211 in two hours, ably assisted by Pawson who scored 57. This turned out to be Ames's last hundred for Kent. After making two more when leading the Commonwealth team in India the following winter, he broke down with back trouble in the first match of the 1951 season and played no more.

Leslie Ames has always been one of the most popular of men. To him, cricket was always a game to be enjoyed; the respect in which he is held can be seen from the number of years he served both Kent and the MCC. At international level he was a selector from 1950 to 1956 and in 1958, and he managed MCC tours abroad. He was Manager of Kent from 1957 to 1960, and then from 1960 to 1974 he combined the duties of Manager and Secretary. He also helped with the coaching, but that wasn't really his scene. In 1975 he became the first ex-professional to be President of Kent, a well-deserved honour. He was also elected a member of the Band of Brothers, only the second professional (Frank Woolley was the other) to have this honour bestowed upon him.

Beyond all doubt, Leslie Ethelbert George Ames, CBE, was the finest wicket-keeper batsman the game has ever known.

William Ashdown

Birthplace:	Bromley, Kent
Born:	27 December 1898
Died:	15 September 1979
Played:	1920-1937

Averages in all first-class Kent matches:

Matches	Innings	Not Outs	Runs	Highest Score	Average	100s
482	804	76	22,309	332	30.64	38

Runs	Wickets	Average	Best Analysis	5wI	10wM	Catches
19,290	595	32.42	6 for 23	12	—	398 (plus 1 st)

Number of Test Appearances: 0

Born in Bromley in 1898, William Henry Ashdown received his grounding in the game at the Kent Nursery at Tonbridge, just before the First World War.

It was in June 1914, when only 15 years old, that he played for G J V Weigall's side against Oxford University, scoring 27 in the second innings.

It was 1921 before he began to make his mark as a very sound batsman. He possessed a wide array of strokes and often bowled at a shade over medium in pace. His bowling was quite useful, usually with the new ball and with an action of a natural games-player. He would make the ball swing away and come quick off the ground. In his best season, 1923, he took 66 wickets at 22.22 runs each.

In 1926, Ashdown scored 1,696 runs at an average of 38.54; it was the start of his partnership with Wally Hardinge, which became the foundation on which the stroke play of Ames and Woolley flourished. With the exception of 1932, Ashdown scored 1,000 runs or more every season from 1926 until 1937. His best season in terms of runs scored was 1928, when he totalled 2,247 runs at an average of 43.21. In 1931, he scored a hundred in each innings against Middlesex at Lord's. He topped the 2,000-run mark again in 1934, the year of his record breaking innings.

His innings of 332 against Essex on a pitch of unnatural ease made out of Kent's 803 for 4, is one that many remember him by. His knock was in the first innings in the first Brentwood Week in 1934. To elaborate further, Kent's total of 803 was made in seven hours five minutes. Ashdown and Fagg put on 70 for the first wicket before Fagg departed and in walked Frank Woolley. He stayed just over three hours, making 172, out just after tea with the score on 422. Les Ames took strike and went on to hit eventually an unbeaten 202. The score at the close of play on that first day was 623 for 2. Whilst all this was going on, Bill Ashdown had unselfishly accumulated 300 runs not out in a day, averaging 50 runs an hour off his own bat. He eventually fell for 332, Kent winning the game by an innings and 192 runs.

The following season Ashdown scored 1,768 runs at an average of 32.74. He almost exceeded his score made in the Essex game, when he carried his bat through an innings of 560 with a faultless 305 made in 6 hours 40 minutes at Dover, with Derbyshire the opponents.

Bill Ashdown also possessed quite a sense of humour. In 1937 when Kent were making 219 in 71 minutes to beat Gloucestershire at Dover, he commented dryly to his partner: 'I suppose you realise you are wasting a lot of time hitting all these sixes!' Ashdown's contribution to this unique cricketing feat was to score 62 not out!

As shown by the 22,309 runs he scored for Kent, he scored heavily in his best seasons. As I mentioned earlier, he did on two occasions play innings of over 300, but he was also a little too inconsistent and prone to spells of failure to be considered for England or other representative teams. Like many batsmen of many eras, he was liable to flash outside the off stump to bowlers of any pace. Yet Ashdown was a beautiful off-driver and cutter, though he could play to leg also, and was often compared with L C H Palairet, the Somerset batsman – a great compliment indeed.

Ashdown took 595 wickets with his useful bowling and 398 catches, mostly taken at slip.

He is also the only player to have played first-class cricket before the First World War and after the Second. Earlier I mentioned his contribution in 1914 when he played for G J V Weigall's side against Oxford University, but he also played in the Harrogate Festival of 1947. He played for Maurice Leyland's XI against The Rest, scoring 42 and 40. He also took 5 for 73 despite hundreds by Brookes and Paynter.

From 1938 to 1947 Ashdown was coach at Rugby, combining the post with being head groundsman. It was a difficult time, but he kept the grounds in tremendous condition during the war. From his position at Rugby, Ashdown moved on to the first-class umpire's panel where he spent three years. He later moved to Grace Road where he was Leicestershire's coach and later scorer.

Bill Ashdown died at his home in Rugby in September 1979 at the age of 80 – the most unselfish and popular of cricketers.

Mark Benson

Birthplace:	Shoreham, Sussex
Born:	6 July 1958
Died:	
Played:	1980-

Averages in all first-class Kent matches:

Matches	Innings	Not Outs	Runs	Highest Score	Average	100s
189	311	26	12,002	162	42.11	31

Runs	Wickets	Average	Best Analysis	5wI	10wM	Catches
378	3	126.00	2 for 55	—	—	91

Number of Test Appearances: 1

Unlike the best primary schools, Mark Benson's school in Caterham did not play cricket! On leaving primary school he spent two years with his family in West Africa and so it was at the age of 13 that he first picked up a cricket bat. This was on his return to England, when he started at Sutton Valence School near Maidstone.

At first, cricket was just one of a number of sports that Benson enjoyed, rugby, hockey and tennis being the others. Benson's father, though, was keen for him to succeed in the game of cricket and sent him to Alf Gover's Indoor School for cricket coaching when he was fourteen years old.

By the following summer the coaching had paid off and Benson had won a place in the school First XI. At the age of 17 he played what was probably his most important game of cricket. He played against the Kent Schools and impressed with the game's top score: 90. He was then chosen for the Kent Schools and later for the Public Schools XI. In 1978 he was taken on to the Kent staff.

In his first year with Kent in 1978 he averaged only 17 for the County Second XI, his top score being just 35. There was no doubt about it, he found an immense gap between cricket at Sutton Valence and cricket in the Second XI of Kent. His future didn't look too rosy and I'm sure he thought he wouldn't make the grade and would be released.

While he was playing for the Second XI, he was also playing an important role in enabling his club side Sevenoaks Vine to win the Kent league. The Kent Committee, though, realised he was playing Second XI County Cricket just a few years after starting the game and kept him on.

In 1979 Benson averaged around 30 runs for the Second XI. The following season he made his debut for the County First XI, scoring a couple of 50s in the few games he played.

In 1981 he started the season with a brisk 81 against Nottinghamshire, following it with his maiden century in the next match against Warwickshire. This was the first season that he passed a thousand runs, scoring 1,083 runs in the Championship at an average of 32.31.

In 1982, despite suffering a bad finger injury halfway through the season, he finished with a County Championship average of 44.00, hitting 1,100 runs. He continued to put together good scores in one-day matches, though in all matches he was moved around the top-half of the batting order. His own favourite position is reported to be at number four, though more often than not, he bats at number three or as an opener.

In 1983 Benson scored 1,515 runs in the Championship at an average of 44.55. In the match against Warwickshire at Edgbaston he scored 102 in the first innings, and 152 not out in the second. Regarded by many in the game of cricket as one of the best players of fast bowling in the country, he is very unfortunate in not having added to his one Test appearance which came in this season. The match was against India at Edgbaston, Benson scoring 21 and 30.

Just before the start of the 1984 season, Benson found himself sidelined with cartilage trouble. He tried to come back a little too soon, but after hitting 130 against Hampshire Second XI and 80 and 100 for his club side Sevenoaks Vine in the Kent league, he was back and played with great spirit after such a frustrating and disappointing start to the season.

In 1985 he scored 1,501 runs at an average of 37.52, including the highest score of his career, 162 made at Southampton against Hampshire. In 1986 he topped a thousand runs again, scoring 1,410 (average 40.28). The following season, in the match at Worcester, he helped Chris Tavare put on 285 for the third wicket. This season, he scored his greatest number of runs in the County Championship: 1,725 at an average of 44.23.

In 1988 he helped Neil Taylor put on 180 against Essex at Canterbury. It was the highest stand for any wicket by Kent in the Benson and Hedges Competition.

Last season he once again topped the thousand-run mark, scoring 1,190 runs (average 54.09). Benson is one of a few Kent players who have scored over twenty centuries for Kent, twenty-eight at present.

He has worked out a very effective way of combating opposing attacks on the county circuit and at the moment, at the age of only thirty-one, I am sure he will be aiming to move up the list of Kent run-getters.

Colin Blythe

Birthplace:	Deptford, London
Born:	30 May 1879
Died:	8 November 1917
Played:	1899-1914

Averages in all first-class Kent matches:

Matches	Innings	Not Outs	Runs	Highest Score	Average	100s
381	506	111	3,964	82*	10.03	—

Runs	Wickets	Average	Best Analysis	5wI	10wM	Catches
36,859	2,210	16.67	10 for 30	195	64	183

Number of Test Appearances: 19

Colin Blythe was discovered at Blackheath, bowling at the nets to Walter Wright. Ex-Kent player, Captain McCanlis, and a member of the county coaching staff liked Blythe's action and actually faced a few balls themselves. They then arranged for a trial at the then recently established Tonbridge Nursery.

Without any hesitation Blythe was taken on, and on 22 August 1899 he played in his first match, against Yorkshire at Tonbridge. With the first ball he bowled in that match he got the wicket of F Mitchell who had already scored 58 runs. That first season saw him take 14 wickets at an average of 22.14 each.

In the fourteen seasons that followed, only once did he fail to take 100 wickets in a season; that was in 1901 when his health was poor. Even then, his tally was 97 wickets, including figures of 6 for 6, 6 for 7, and 5 for 10 on wickets which were helpful to him. He visited Australia with a team captained by Lancashire's Archie MacLaren in 1901-02 and never looked back. In 1902 he took 127 wickets, his best analysis being 8 for 42 against Somerset at Maidstone. In 1903 he claimed 142 wickets at 13.75 each, including 9 for 67 against Essex at Canterbury.

The next three seasons saw him take 398 wickets, with Hampshire being the county to suffer most. In 1904 he had match figures of 13 for 91 at Southampton (including 9 for 30 in the first innings), following it up with 15 for 76 at Tonbridge.

In May 1907 he accomplished the remarkable performance of taking 10 wickets in an innings and 17 in a match – all in one day at Northampton. At one time Northamptonshire were 4 runs for 7 wickets, Blythe actually having got 7 Northamptonshire wickets for one run! They managed to make 60 in their first innings, faring even worse in the second, when they were all out for 39. Blythe emerged as the conquering hero with 10 for 30 and 7 for 18, all in less than a day's play during 31.1 overs.

In the same season he played in all three Tests against the famous South African team. The first and third Test matches were drawn. The second Test at Headingley was a different affair on a pitch that was affected by rain. England were dismissed for 76, whilst South Africa could only muster 110, Blythe taking 8 for 59. In their second innings England made 162, leaving South Africa to get 129 to win. They didn't stand a chance as Blythe never bowled a loose delivery, finishing with 7 for 40 and were all out for 75.

Altogether that season Blythe took 183 wickets at an average of 15.42 runs each.

Harry Altham described Blythe as a 'highly sensitive and nervous instrument beautifully co-ordinated, directed by a subtle mind and inspired by a natural love of its art'.

'Charlie' as he was always called, was a very accomplished violinist – there was certainly something of this in his bowling. His long, sensitive musician's fingers enabled him to spin the ball and make it leap from the pitch, as if the ball were alive. On a sticky wicket, or on a dry pitch, the ball would come off the ground with far more pace than the batsman imagined. In fact the ball that went with the arm often approached the speed of a fast bowler!

As a complete contrast to his love for the violin, he would also willingly pay five guineas to see a good fight!

Blythe found games for Kent no trouble, but it is reported that he found that Test matches 'got on his nerves'. The series against Australia in 1909 and especially the match at Edgbaston was a prime example. In that match Blythe took 11 for 102, but on his return to Kent a medical specialist advised the county club that he shouldn't play in the next Test at Lord's. His diagnosis was that 'he suffers in a peculiar way from the strain on his nervous system caused by playing in a Test match'. Instead of playing at Lord's he continued to represent Kent, taking 36 wickets in the space of twelve days. In the game against Warwickshire after taking 9 for 123, he had to leave the field, feeling unwell, suffering what was described as an epileptic fit.

His best season was 1909 when he took in first-class matches, 215 wickets at a cost of 14.54 runs each. In one day at Leicester he took 14 for 56 (including 9 for 42 in the first innings). His other top performance that season included 8 for 49 against Derbyshire, and 9 for 44 against Northamptonshire.

Blyth also fancied himself as a batsman, for he could certainly hit. In 1906 he got 53 in 35 minutes from a ninth-wicket partnership of 119. Against Somerset he scored 70 out of 98 added for the last wicket. Yet when he first attended the Tonbridge Nursery it was said that his batting technique left a lot to be desired!

His last great performance with the ball was his 9 for 97 in the county fixture against Surrey. The game was played at Lord's and was Jack Hobbs's benefit match. Unfortunately Kent were dismissed for 140 in both innings, and Surrey won in two days.

His final flourish on the cricket field was made in the game in which the man who was eventually to replace him as the county's leading bowler was making his County Championship debut – 'Tich' Freeman.

In his career Blythe took 2,509 wickets at an average of 16.80 runs each. He took 10 wickets in a match on fifty occasions and 13 wickets or more in a match fifteen times.

In 1914 he was bowling as well as ever and for the third year running he topped the first-class bowling averages. Yet, despite his physical disability, he was one of the first cricket professionals to join up. Sometime in 1917 Sgt Colin Blythe announced that he was taking up a coaching appointment at Eton and he would retire from County cricket. Those plans never came to fruition. He was killed in November of that year by a shell, after being drafted to the Western Front.

Before the year was out the Kent club had determined to erect a memorial to Colin Blythe, a man who was universally loved and respected, but it had to wait until the First World War was over.

Walter Bradley

Birthplace:	Sydenham, London
Born:	2 February 1875
Died:	19 June 1944
Played:	1895-1903

Averages in all first-class Kent matches:

Matches	Innings	Not Outs	Runs	Highest Score	Average	100s
123	185	50	795	67*	5.88	—

Runs	Wickets	Average	Best Analysis	5wI	10wM	Catches
11,886	536	22.17	9 for 87	39	10	71

Number of Test Appearances: 2

Walter Morris Bradley, or 'Bill' as he became known, was born in Sydenham and attended the Alleyn's School where he played for the First XI. He also played for Lloyd's Register, doing remarkable things. In one match against Mitcham he took 6 wickets with consecutive balls. He was tried for Kent and became a protege of Lord Harris.

Bill Bradley was a fast bowler, with a long run and unusual action. He would start his run from somewhere behind mid-on, relying on lift and pace for his wickets. He used to get through a great deal and was a super trier. He would pitch at the stumps, very rarely bowling short. His spells were often long but, no matter how long he bowled, there was no slackening in his speed.

He made his debut for Kent in 1895, but it was some four years later before he made his mark. In that year of 1899, in the County Championship, Bradley took 129 wickets at a cost of 17.91 runs each. He also performed the hat-trick on two occasions, the first against Essex at Leyton, the second against Yorkshire at Tonbridge.

Also in 1899, he represented England on two occasions against the Australians. England's team contained some great players – Ranjitsinhji, Fry, Rhodes, and MacLaren the captain. The game at Old Trafford was proof of his ability to bowl spells without losing his pace. Joe Darling's Australia were faced with Bradley's pace for the first time. His great efforts brought him the figures of 5 for 67 in 33 overs. Under the Laws of that time, Australia had to follow on. Bill Bradley went on to bowl a further 46 overs in Australia's second innings! There is no doubt about it, the Law was a ludicrous one. After his good performance at Old Trafford he kept his place for the next Test at the Oval. Unfortunately, he met with no success there and didn't represent his country again. He took 6 Test wickets at a cost of 38.83 runs each.

In all matches that season his victims totalled 156 at an average of 19.10 each – he was the best amateur bowler that year. His best performances that season came against Nottinghamshire at Trent Bridge when he took 12 for 83. In 1900 he performed the hat-trick for the third time against Somerset at Blackheath.

In 1901 Bradley took 112 wickets in the County Championship at an average of 23.16 runs each. Some of his better performances came against Lancashire at Old Trafford, where he had match figures of 14 for 134 and against Surrey at Canterbury, where he took 12 wickets for 142. This was also the season of his best bowling analysis, when he took 9 for 87 against Hampshire at Tonbridge.

As a batsman, like most number elevens, he wasn't really expected to score runs. But in 1897, in the match against Yorkshire at Canterbury, he had his day. He and Walter Wright put on 95 runs in three-quarters of an hour, Bradley's share being 67 not out.

Altogether in his nine seasons of first-class cricket (his last season being 1903) he took 624 wickets at 22.64 runs each, scored 906 runs at an average of 6.09 and took 77 catches.

For around thirty years afterwards, he played club cricket, always having a kind word of encouragement for the youngsters in his team.

In the last few years of his life, which coincided with the Second World War, he would wear his MCC tie and visit the Long Room at Lord's to talk over past matches. He died in June 1944, aged 69, and was buried within a short distance of W G Grace at Elmer's End Cemetery.

Cuthbert Burnup

Birthplace:	Blackheath, London
Born:	21 November 1875
Died:	5 April 1960
Played:	1896-1907

Averages in all first-class Kent matches:

Matches	Innings	Not Outs	Runs	Highest Score	Average	100s
157	271	17	9,668	200	38.06	20

Runs	Wickets	Average	Best Analysis	5wI	10wM	Catches
1,795	41	43.78	5 for 44	1	—	74

Number of Test Appearances: 0

Cuthbert James Burnup attended Malvern School where, from 1892, he played for three years in the First XI. He then moved on to Cambridge University, playing on a regular basis from 1896 to 1898. His best season, without doubt, was his first in 1896 when he scored 666 runs in just 9 matches. At Lord's that season in the match against Oxford University, he scored 80 and 11. Though Burnup played against Oxford on three occasions, that match in 1896 was notable for two occurances. W G Grace, Junior, son of the great man, failed to score in both Cambridge innings. Cambridge bowler, E B Shine, acting on his captain's orders, deliberately bowled three balls to the boundary to prevent Oxford following on! It was in 1896 that Burnup made his county debut for Kent, but a further three years before he made his mark.

C.J.BURNUP.

34

In 1899 Burnup scored 1,557 runs in the County Championship at an average of 44.48. He carried his bat in the match against Surrey at the Oval, scoring 103 not out in Kent's total of 209.

Though Burnup wasn't thought of as a bowler, he had one great success with the ball that summer. When Australia, led by Joseph Darling, visited Canterbury they found Burnup swinging the ball a great deal. He took 3 for 7 in their first innings and 5 for 44 in the second.

In 1900 Burnup scored 1,160 runs at an average of 32.22. During this season he made the highest score of his career, 200 against Lancashire at Old Trafford. At that time it was also the highest ever made for Kent. The following season he once again topped 1,000 runs, but in 1902 he was to have his best season.

He scored 1,440 runs that season in County Championship matches, but in all games he scored 2,048 runs at an average of 39.38.

In County Championship matches he exceeded 1,000 runs in six seasons. He had a busy style, tending to score runs quicker than the spectator realised. As an opening batsman, Burnup could score quickly when it was necessary. He played well off his legs, though he favoured the cut and off-drive. His stance was similar to Gilbert Jessop of Gloucestershire: holding the bat low, he would await delivery in a crouched position.

As a fielder Burnup was one of the fastest on the county circuit and with a safe pair of hands.

He took part in tours to Australia, New Zealand, Holland and America (twice).

Like other players of his generation, he was a good soccer player, representing Cambridge from 1895 to 1898. He was also a soccer international, playing for England against Scotland in 1896, though the majority of his games were for the Corinthians.

Burnup was extremely unlucky in that he didn't play at international level at cricket. The nearest he came to it was to play for the Gentlemen against the Players. This he did on six occasions, hitting 123 at the Oval on his first appearance.

In 1903 he captained Kent and continued to do so until they captured the County Championship in 1906. In that Championship winning year Burnup scored 1,207 runs at an average of 67.05.

When he retired from the first-class scene the following year, 1907, Burnup's career average was 37.85, higher than that of any other regular player.

Douglas Carr

Birthplace:	Cranbrook, Kent	
Born:	17 March 1872	
Died:	23 March 1950	
Played:	1909-1914	

Averages in all first-class Kent matches:

Matches	Innings	Not Outs	Runs	Highest Score	Average	100s
49	54	13	398	48	9.70	—

Runs	Wickets	Average	Best Analysis	5wI	10wM	Catches
4,529	290	15.61	8 for 36	27	8	18

Number of Test Appearances: 1

Douglas Ward Carr was born at Cranbrook in March 1872. He attended the Sutton Valence School and from there went on to Braesnose College, Oxford. Whilst at the University he played little cricket because of an injury to his knee, picked up playing football.

On leaving the city of dreaming spires he moved to Kent, where he played club cricket for Mote Park, the Free Foresters and the Band of Brothers. By 1908 he had gained the ability to bowl both the googly and the leg-break and was an outstanding success in club cricket. Sometimes he would bowl the googly, other times fast-medium. He was very impressed by Bosanquet and the South Africans and found that when he began to experiement with the googly, he lost his leg-break.

Soon he attracted the county club's attention. At the age of 37 he made his Kent debut in 1909 against a not-too-strong Oxford University side. He took 7 wickets in the match, including 5 for 65 in the first innings. On the strength of this one match he was asked to play for the Gentlemen against the Players. At Lord's he had match figures of 8 for 138, and at the Oval 7 for 128. His County Championship debut for Kent came later that year, when he took 6 for 85 against Essex at Leyton. In the seven Championship matches he played that season, he took 51 wickets. He was invited that season to Old Trafford for the Test match against Australia. He was left out because the ground was soft.

But at the Oval, after three further good performances for Kent, he was chosen to represent his country. His captain, Archie MacLaren of Lancashire, was heavily criticised in some quarters for bowling Carr into the ground – he finished with 5 for 146 in the first innings and took 2 further wickets in the second. His victims included Gregory, Armstrong (twice),

Noble and Trumper. It had been a gamble by MacLaren to go into the game without a fast bowler. Carr was his secret weapon and, for a time, it worked. Carr never played for his country again, neither did poor MacLaren.

At the end of that season he took 8 for 105 for Lord Londesborough's XI against the Australians, helping to win the game. For his performances during the season he was chosen as one of Wisden's Five Cricketers of the Year.

Carr, a schoolmaster, continued to play county cricket for Kent during the holidays. He pushed through low-arm accurate, bouncing leg-breaks and googlies, continuing to make even the best batsmen struggle. Despite only playing for the month of August, he contributed greatly to Kent winning the Championship three times in five years.

He showed that his entry into first-class cricket was no fluke. In 1910, he topped the Kent bowling averages. Even though he only played the last month or so, he took 60 wickets in Championship matches at an average of 12.16 runs each.

He continued this good form up to 1914, when the war intervened and he dropped out of the first-class game. He had another successful year in 1912, taking 49 wickets at 9.59 runs each.

In the six seasons that he played county cricket for Kent, he took 334 wickets in all games at an average of 16.84 runs each. He showed the Kent Committee the value of a leg-break and googly bowler and was probably instrumental in them signing 'Tich' Freeman.

Towards the end of the 1914 season, in the game against Surrey at Blackheath, he was taken apart by Tom Hayward and Jack Hobbs. At the age of 42, the county no longer required his services but he had enjoyed a late and remarkable career.

A unique cricketer, Douglas Carr died in a nursing home at Sidmouth, Devon, in 1950 at the age of 78.

Gerry Chalk

Birthplace:	Sydenham, London
Born:	7 September 1910
Died:	17 February 1943
Played:	1933-1939

Averages in all first-class Kent matches:

Matches	Innings	Not Outs	Runs	Highest Score	Average	100s
101	169	12	4,436	198	28.25	5

Runs	Wickets	Average	Best Analysis	5wI	10wM	Catches
137	2	68.50	2 for 25	—	—	40

Number of Test Appearances: 0

Frederick Gerald Hudson Chalk was born in London in 1910, playing his early cricket at Uppingham School. In 1928 he topped his school batting averages with 44.00. He moved up to Oxford University where he gained his Blue as a Braesnose Freshman in 1931. When Chalk first played against Cambridge, Oxford won by 8 wickets, the following three encounters all being drawn. Therefore, he never appeared on the losing side in Oxford-Cambridge confrontations. His best performance came in the 1934 match, when he hit a magnificent 108 at Lord's.

38

After finishing Oxford in 1934 he played the remainder of the season for Kent, averaging 38.84 with the bat. On coming down from Oxford, Chalk spent a couple of years as a master at Malvern and so his scholastic duties somewhat limited his number of games for Kent.

Chalk had a very skilful defence but he could also score at every available opportunity, making him a valuable asset to have at your disposal. As a neat, tidy player, he played shots on both sides of the wicket. His speed and accuracy as an off-side fielder kept up the reputation that the Kent amateur players had maintained for many years.

In 1937, whilst still not devoting his entire time to Kent cricket, he scored a superb 107 in a fighting innings at Lord's against Middlesex. He cut, drove and pulled his way to a century on a badly worn pitch. His innings consisted of three sixes and ten fours.

It wasn't until 1938 that Gerry Chalk was available for a full season and then he was made captain. He made 1,057 runs at an average of 24.58, also sharing with Arthur Fagg in a second wicket stand of 275 against Worcestershire at Dudley.

In 1939 he scored 1,288 runs at an average of 30.66. His highest score of 198 against Sussex at Tonbridge was made this season though, probably, his greatest effort came in the match against Yorkshire at Dover, just a week before the outbreak of the Second World War. Kent were forced to follow-on and in their second innings were dismissed for 215. Despite losing the match, the one bright spot was Gerry Chalk's knock of 115 not out, carrying his bat through the innings. Five days later Kent were set 382 to win by Lancashire. They won by five wickets with an hour or so to spare. They got off to a flying start with Fagg and Chalk putting on 181 for the first wicket, Chalk's contribution being 94.

Gerry Chalk was a good captain, getting the best out of all his players. He handled the bowlers in a shrewd way and was always pressing for victory. In the 27 games that Kent played that season, only three of them were drawn.

There is little doubt that Gerry Chalk had not reached his best when the Second World War came. He joined the Honourable Artillery Company as a gunner before transferring to th RAF as a rear gunner. In June 1941 he won the DFC when returning from an air raid on Hanover. It was described officially thus: 'Chalk by his cool and accurate fire undoubtedly saved his aircraft and probably destroyed the attacker – an Me 110.' Chalk then took a pilot's course and was promoted to Flight Lieutenant, later becoming a Spitfire Flight Commander.

Chalk was also a fine pianist who played by ear and could not read a line of music!

He went missing from February 1943 and in January 1944 was officially 'presumed killed'.

Flight Lieutenant Gerry Chalk's tragic death at the age of only 32 was a tremendous blow to Kent County Cricket Club.

Percy Chapman

Birthplace: Reading, Berkshire
Born: 3 September 1900
Died: 16 September 1961
Played: 1924-1938

Averages in all first-class Kent matches:

Matches	Innings	Not Outs	Runs	Highest Score	Average	100s
194	269	21	6,681	260	26.93	8

Runs	Wickets	Average	Best Analysis	5wI	10wM	Catches
151	3	50.33	2 for 24	—	—	173

Number of Test Appearances: 26

Arthur Percy Frank Chapman was born in Reading and attended the Uppingham School. He was in the First XI for four years, from 1916-19, the last two as captain. In 1917 he topped the school batting averages, scoring 668 runs in just 10 innings and an average of 111.33. He didn't start the season well at all, but he ended with scores of 66, 206, 160, 81 and 114. He was not out on four occasions and run out on the other!

His adventurous left-handed batting and fielding won him a Blue at Cambridge, as a freshman. This wasn't too surprising, especially as on his first-class debut he'd taken 118 off the Essex attack at Fenners. Against Oxford in 1920 he scored 27 and was chosen for the Gentlemen at Lord's. The following year he scored 45 against Oxford and then in 1922 he scored a brilliant 102 not out to help Cambridge to a comfortable victory. He followed this up by making 160 in the Gentlemen v Player fixture. He was also a member of Archie MacLaren's legendary side which beat the Australians at Eastbourne by 28 runs.

Chapman had been playing well for Berkshire in Minor County cricket but in 1924 he qualified for Kent by taking a job in Mackeson's Brewery in Hythe. He was one of the few players to play for England while still playing Minor County cricket. His England debut was in 1924 against South Africa at home, followed by the trip to Australia under A E R Gilligan. From then onwards he was a permanent fixture in the England team. He captained his country on 17 occasions, winning 9 and losing only 2.

In 1926 he shared in the Kent fourth wicket record partnership of 297 with Wally Hardinge in the match against Hampshire at Southampton. He only played in nine games that season. However, he was to become a national hero – he led England to victory at the Oval, so the Ashes were regained.

A.P.F.CHAPMAN.   KE   C.FLEMONS.TONBRIDGE.

42

Chapman's greatest innings came in 1927. Kent were playing the champions Lancashire at Maidstone. When he marched to the wicket Kent were struggling at 70 for 5, with Hardinge, Ashdown, A J Evans, Woolley and Ames back in the pavilion. Percy Chapman and Geoff Legge added 284 in two-and-a-half hours. Legge's contribution was 101, but it was Chapman with 260 who turned it Kent's way. He counter-attacked against the great Australian bowler in Lancashire's ranks, Ted McDonald, still one of the world's fastest, and the spinner Dick Tyldesley. Chapman hit five sixes and thirty-two fours in his incredible innings.

He only hit one century for England, 121 against Australia at Lord's in 1930. With that, he achieved a triple performance never before accomplished. He had previously hit hundreds for Cambridge and then in 1922 for the Gentlemen against the Players, a match in which Chapman made nineteen appearances.

Chapman captained Kent from 1931 to 1936 and in his twenty-six appearances for England he was captain on seventeen occasions. He was one of the most popular and successful of England's captains. As captain of Kent he was often criticised as not being a great tactician. However, there is one thing that is certain – all those who played under Percy at Kent were happy and cheerful, for he was generous and carefree in character. He was also a superb cutter and driver who liked nothing better than lifting the ball. If it was delivered outside his off-stump it may well have gone for six over cover or even third man!

In his entire career, Chapman scored 16,309 runs at an average of 31.97. Figures, however, don't give a true picture of this hard-hitting batsman, who could turn a game as quickly as any cricketer of his generation or since.

He was a superb fielder for Kent and England, usually close to the bat and mostly at gully and silly mid-off. Chapman was accused of not being tactically aware, but he did have a shrewd cricket brain and wasn't afraid to ask for advice, notably from Jack Hobbs. He was extremely popular and when he was dropped from the England team for the last Test in 1930, the decision was widely condemned.

Percy Chapman was friendly with everyone. After the Second World War his life went into sad eclipse. His health grew so bad that he couldn't get to Lord's or Canterbury to watch the game he loved so much. He died in Alton Hospital, Hampshire, aged 61, a player who will always be remembered for his great personal charm.

George Collins

Birthplace:	Gravesend, Kent
Born:	29 October 1889
Died:	23 January 1949
Played:	1911-1928

Averages in all first-class Kent matches:

Matches	Innings	Not Outs	Runs	Highest Score	Average	100s
212	316	37	6,237	110	22.35	4

Runs	Wickets	Average	Best Analysis	5wI	10wM	Catches
8,964	378	23.71	10 for 65	24	3	79 (plus 1 st)

Number of Test Appearances: 0

George Collins was born at Gravesend where he learned his cricket. He later played at Cobham where his family had close ties. His father, Christopher, and his uncle, George, played for Kent in the early 1880s. Christopher Collins retired from the Kent side at the age of 25 as his action was suspect, but had the honour of playing for Cobham under the captaincy of the Hon Ivo Bligh, Eighth Earl of Darnley, who captained England on their successful trip to Australia in 1882.

George Collins attended the Tonbridge Nursery under the great coach Captain McCanlis before making his Kent debut in 1911. He played only occasionally before the war, producing some brave innings, but as there seemed little chance of a regular spot in the Kent First XI, he left the staff.

However, in 1919 things were different and Collins returned to the Kent staff. He was to do good service until the 1928 season.

As a batsman Collins was a clumsy left-hander, but was both adaptable and unselfish. He was equally prepared to open the batting early in the season with Wally Hardinge then, as the season wore on and the batting line-up stronger, he would bat at number seven or eight. George Collins was a very courageous batsman and a great trier. If a more capable batsman in the first six for Kent needed someone to keep an end closed up, George would readily volunteer and do his best to stop there without worrying about scoring runs. In fact, probably most of his innings were made when Kent were in trouble.

In 1924 Kent were playing Yorkshire at Hull and trying to bat out for a draw. George Collins played a ball down to Maurice Leyland fielding at short-leg, who took it low to the ground, claiming a catch. The umpire was unsighted and went to discuss the appeal with his colleague. The

Yorkshire team joined in the discussion, expressing their view in no uncertain terms. George, a friendly yet simple soul, left his crease to put forward his opinion. A Yorkshireman then removed the bails saying: 'You're out now' – the umpire, however, declared the catch a good one. When the matter was reported to Lord Harris, there was certainly no sympathy for George Collins.

Collins's best season with the bat was 1923 when he scored 1,036 runs at an average of 22.04. Altogether in first-class cricket, he scored 6,270 runs at an average of 22.15. In 1925-26 he visited the West Indies as a member of the MCC team.

As a bowler he was right-handed, taking a long bounding run, but the end product was a little disappointing, his deliveries never exceeding fast-medium. He would often capture valuable wickets early in the innings and certainly surprised one or two of the stronger county sides as he ran through them.

Perhaps the best example of this occurred at Dover in 1922 when Nottinghamshire were the visitors. In the first innings he took 6 for 18, following it with all ten wickets in the second, 10 for 65. Despite his huge frame and his ability to lift a pavilion chair in his teeth and hold it parallel to the ground, he was rather a slow mover!

In this match, when he'd taken 9 wickets, he had the chance to catch a ball from 'Tich' Freeman's bowling that would have been the tenth wicket. He was slow to move to it, and when he got there he couldn't hold on to it. He was greatly upset, suspecting that the crowd would think he'd dropped it on purpose. The following over, it was Freeman who took a brilliant catch to provide Collins with all 10 wickets. He finished the season with 75 wickets at 18.62 runs each. He would bowl a superb length, the ball breaking back quickly off the ground. Having said this, on one occasion against Middlesex, he bowled four consecutive wides!

Altogether he took 379 first-class wickets at 23.60 runs each.

On his retirement from first-class cricket he was, for many years, groundsman to the Officer's Club at Aldershot. A simple but friendly man, he died in January 1949, aged 59.

Colin Cowdrey

Birthplace:	Octacamund, India
Born:	24 December 1932
Died:	
Played:	1950-1976

Averages in all first-class Kent matches:

Matches	Innings	Not Outs	Runs	Highest Score	Average	100s
402	651	85	23,779	250	42.01	58

Runs	Wickets	Average	Best Analysis	5wI	10wM	Catches
1,285	27	47.59	4 for 22	—	—	406

Number of Test Appearances: 114

Michael Colin Cowdrey was born in Octacamund, India where, after his birth, his cricketing father's enthusiasm for the game led him to give his son the initials MCC. In fact, his father was top scorer for the Europeans against the 1926-27 touring team in India.

In March 1938 the Cowdrey family was sailing back from India to England when young Colin was dragged from his bunk and shown a passing ship which was bringing the Australian team to try to beat England. Colin's father told him that Don Bradman was on board – from then on, young Colin's thoughts were firmly on the game of cricket.

On his arrival in England he attended the Homefield Preparatory School in Surrey, where the Headmaster, Charles Walford, began to coach him in cricket technique. In 1945 he was sent to Gover's School; Alf Gover himself wrote to the Tonbridge coach, Ewart Astill, telling him to expect a 13-year-old good enough to play in the First XI. This proved to be true and school rules were bent, as at the age of 13 he went to Lord's to play against Clifton. Cowdrey was classed as a leg-spin bowler and would bat at number three. He was the youngest player to take part in a public schools' match at Lord's. In the first innings he scored 75, which was more than half his side's runs from the bat, following it up with 44 out of 175 in the second. As a bowler he took 3 for 58 in their first innings and then just as Clifton looked likey to win, he took their last 5 wickets for 33 to help Tonbridge win the match by two runs. For the next five years he was to dominate cricket at Tonbridge School. He was so successful that he was chosen to captain the Public Schools XI against the Combined Services and scored a century.

At the age of 17 he was in the Kent side, and within two years he had been capped, the youngest in Kent's history. He had also scored centuries for the Free Foresters and the Gentlemen in their match against the Players.

He went up to Oxford, where he was a prolific scorer and a Blue for three years. He hit a hundred in the Varsity match and was captain in his last year.

In 1953 Cowdrey hit a century against Surrey at the Oval on a wicket perfectly suited to Surrey's spin twins, Laker and Lock. He scored 154 out of Kent's 270, following it with 34 in the second innings, as Kent were shot out for 63, Laker taking 8 wickets in the match.

In September 1954 Cowdrey was part of the MCC touring party which set sail from Tilbury bound for Australia. Wisden reported the event: 'M C Cowdrey was given a place although he had not approached his splendid form of the previous year.' Cowdrey, in fact, had been selected on the strength of having made two fifties against the Australians for the Gentlemen at Lord's a year earlier, while he was still at Oxford. Among the crowd on the Tilbury dockside was Cowdrey's father; his sudden death when Colin was in Australia was a great shock for him. He had had only one full season in county cricket and therefore felt a little out of it, as he didn't know too many of the players.

He batted quite usefully in the first two Tests and hit two hundreds in the match against New South Wales, but it was in the third Test at Melbourne that he produced one of the finest innings seen in a Test match. England were 41 for 4, with Edrich, May, Hutton and Compton back in

the tent, as he made his way out to the middle. He went on to make 102 out of an 'all out' total of 191. He put his bat to the ball, his body over and sometimes behind it. His hundred in front of the vast 63,000 crowd saved the English performance from complete humiliation. Australia replied to England's total with 231. England scored 279 (May 91) in their second innings and then Frank Tyson (7 for 27) bowled Australia out for 111 and they were beaten by 128 runs.

He returned to England to again score freely and although he didn't reach a thousand runs for the season in the County Championship, he scored two unbeaten hundreds, 115 not out and 103 not out in the match against Essex at Gillingham.

In 1956 he scored 1,292 runs at an average of 43.06, his highest score being 204 not out against Cambridge University. It was the first of thirteen times in the County Championship that he was to pass the thousand-run mark, but twenty-two times in all matches. He also carried his bat for 65 out of Kent's total of 169 that season. At Edgbaston in 1957 came the turning point in Cowdrey's development as a major Test batsman. He scored 154 against the West Indies, as he and Peter May put on 411 for the fourth wicket in eight hours twenty minutes. It was really the first time that he had scored a Test hundred by occupation of the crease rather than by his usual magnificent stroke-play. It was an innings that laid the Ramadhin bogey, as he played forward, padding the ball away, over after over. Ramadhin appealed with great regularity for lbw, but there was little chance, for Cowdrey was a long way down the pitch.

His highest Kent aggregate came in 1959, when he scored 1,613 runs for an average of 50.40. It included his biggest county score, 250 against Essex at Blackheath. During the MCC tour of the West Indies in 1959-60 Cowdrey played as an opener and had a wonderful time. He faced the terrifyingly fast new-ball attack of Hall and Watson. His hooking of Wes Hall was brilliant. In ten innings he scored 491 runs at an average of 54.55. His scores included 114 and 97 (in the same match) and 119. There followed another example of his masterful stroke-play in the 1960 home series against South Africa. Neil Adcock, South Africa's hostile opening bowler, had already caused England plenty of problems and dismissed Cowdrey five times in the series already, but not this time, as Cowdrey went on to score 155 and so help England avoid defeat.

In 1961 he scored 1,239 runs (average 59.00), producing probably the greatest of his performances for Kent in their match against the Australians at Canterbury. He was at his best as he scored 149 and 121. At the end of the game Kent needed only 8 runs to gain their first win against the Australians since 1899.

The highest score of his career, 307, was made for the MCC team when they played South Australia in 1962-63. In 1963 his arm was broken in the Lord's Test in mid-June and that was the end of his season. However, he bounced back the following summer, scoring 1,562 runs at an average of 57.85.

Probably his best English season was 1965, when he headed Kent's batting averages in the Championship: 1,230 runs at an average of 64.73. He took hundreds off both the touring sides, 119 against New Zealand and 105 against South Africa.

In 1967-68 Cowdrey captained England when they toured the West Indies. He batted magnificently on that tour and his innings of 71 at Port of Spain won the Test. It was a piece of beautifully controlled batting. The following summer saw Colin play in his hundredth Test match against the Australians at Edgbaston. To celebrate this achievement, he hit yet another Test century. The England captaincy cannot really have helped his peace of mind, though he insists that the distractions of the captaincy never affected him. The selection, though, of Yorkshire's Ray Illingworth to captain the England tour to Australia in 1970-71 caused him some upset; before accepting the vice-captaincy he hesitated and unfortunately never reproduced his true form on that trip.

One morning in December 1974 Colin Cowdrey's usual morning routine was shattered by a phone call from Mike Denness in Australia. The England captain went on to explain that injuries had ravaged the touring party and that he and the rest of the players wanted Colin to fly out and join them in their battle against Lillee and Thomson. These bowlers had already broken one of Dennis Amiss's thumbs and one of John Edrich's hands. Further injuries meant that Colin marched in at number three to face Lillee and Thomson in the second Test at Perth, only three days after landing there. Colin was only 42, but the Australian press greeted him as though it was Methuselah who was to face the onslaught. His jovial reply was 'Why should I worry? After all, I faced Gregory and McDonald!' In the first innings he went in first wicket down and scored 22; in the second he had to open after Brian Luckhurst broke a hand, and scored 41.

His last century against the Australians came the following season at Canterbury. Kent were chasing 354 to win. Cowdrey, with his match-winning innings of 151 not out, steered Kent to victory by 4 wickets. It was a vintage Cowdrey innings; he certainly got his own back for the treatment he received some six months earlier. At the age of 43 he was hooking the ferocious Lillee in front of square! He had already decided to retire at the end of this season and this innings was a fitting finale.

He made twenty-two Test centuries; only Sobers, Boycott, Bradman and Gavaskar made more. He currently stands at tenth in the list of all-time run-scorers with 42,719. He hit 107 first-class hundreds, a batsman who possessed every shot in the book. He has won all the game's honours except for the MCC captaincy in Australia, for which he has been four times a candidate. He toured 'Down Under' six times between 1954-55 and 1974-75. He has also played in more Tests and Test innings and held more catches than any other player.

He was awarded the CBE for his services to the game and made a member of the MCC Committee. Two of his sons went on to play for Kent; Chris also captaining England as well as his county, and Graham showing plenty of potential.

In 1986 Colin Cowdrey's appointment as MCC President for the club's bicentenary in 1987 was well received by all connected with Kent cricket. He was a true sportsman, charming, gentle and friendly. He was true to himself and to the game he loved, the ideal and happy cricketer for Kent and England.

Mike Denness

Birthplace:	Bellshill, Lanark
Born:	1 December 1940
Died:	
Played:	1962-1976

Averages in all first-class Kent matches:

Matches	Innings	Not Outs	Runs	Highest Score	Average	100s
333	562	44	17,047	178	32.90	21

Runs	Wickets	Average	Best Analysis	5wI	10wM	Catches
55	2	27.50	1 for 7	—	—	308

Number of Test Appearances: 28

Michael Henry Denness was born at Bellshill, near Glasgow. At the age of 7 his family moved to Ayr, where he was to learn his cricket. At school his sports lesson was only a short one, so Denness picked up tips by watching established players on televised matches.

At the age of 8 he joined the junior team at the Ayr Cricket Club, where he would spend hours on the ground and at the nets. The coach at Ayr was Charlie Oakes, the old Sussex player, and Denness developed his style and timing under his guidance.

Eventually Denness made his way into the Ayr First XI, where his consistent batting was noticed. In 1959 he was the first schoolboy to be capped by Scotland, making his debut against Ireland. Playing in these games was the former Kent all-rounder, Jim Allan. It was probably on Allan's recommendation that Les Ames invited Denness for a month's trial in 1961.

In 1962 he joined Kent on a special registration, appearing for the first time in July against Essex. It was unfortunate that he had to face Jim Laker on a turning wicket and scored 0 in the first innings and only 3 in the second. In the next game against Surrey, he top-scored with 51.

In 1963 Denness topped the thousand runs in a season for the first time, scoring 1,098 runs at an average of 33.27. In the mid-sixties Denness continued to pass the thousand runs in County Championship matches, his highest score in that period being 174 made at Folkestone in the match against Derbyshire. In 1966 he scored 1,534 runs (average 32.63). It was in that season that his decisive batting on the notorious Bath wicket, when he scored 97 and 87, helped Kent to a 164-run win over Somerset.

In 1967 Denness once again topped the thousand-run mark, also winning the Man-of-the-Match award, as Kent defeated Somerset in the Gillette Cup Final. The following year Denness scored over 1,500 runs in the Championship, forming arguably the best opening pair in the country with Brian Luckhurst. In fact, that season, they scored 3,000 runs between them.

1969 was a very important year for Mike Denness; he took over the captaincy of the county in May, after Colin Cowdrey had suffered an Achilles tendon injury that was to keep him out until the last game of the season. It was also the season that he made his England debut in the Test series against the West Indies.

When Kent won the County Championship in their centenary year, Denness stepped in efficiently to lead the side when Cowdrey was on Test match duty. It didn't affect his batting as he scored 1,494 runs at an average of 40.37. Against Essex, Denness scored 167 on the opening day, leading Kent to a fine win. He followed this with a victory over Hampshire at Maidstone and then, when Cowdrey returned, he hit another hundred in the defeat of Somerset. Prior to these three matches, Kent had stood bottom of the table and the season was half over! Against Gloucestershire he scored a brilliant 97, batting at the peak of his power to enable Kent to reach an almost impossible target of 340 on a bad wicket. This season also saw Denness and Luckhurst put on 182 for the first wicket at Weston-super-Mare against Somerset – still the highest Sunday League stand for Kent.

In 1971 Kent totalled only three fewer points than when they won the County Championship, yet finished in fourth place. Denness again scored 1,494 runs at an average of 38.30. He had taken over the captaincy a season earlier than had been planned and as he did not always open the innings, it meant the end of the brilliant partnership he had established with Brian Luckhurst. At one stage that season Kent were well in the running for the Championship, but a big factor was the injury to Denness, who broke his nose in the two-run defeat by Sussex at Eastbourne. This season saw Denness, when he did open the batting, carry his bat for 69 out of Kent's 136 against Northamptonshire at Wellingborough.

In 1972 Mike Denness had the satisfaction of leading Kent to their first Sunday League title, in what was his first full season as captain.

In 1972-73 he toured India, Pakistan and Sri Lanka as vice-captain, playing skilfully against the Indian spinners. His best form, however, was shown in the next two tours, when he captained his country. In the Caribbean he helped in some remarkable recoveries, as England drew the series against a much stronger West Indies team. His batting limitations, like those of the other England players in the 1974-75 tour of Australia, were exposed by the magnificent bowling of Lillee and Thomson. In fact, Denness dropped himself for the fourth Test at Sydney in which Australia regained the Ashes. He returned for the last Test at Melbourne, scoring a brilliant 188 and averaged 54 overall.

In 1973, under Denness's leadership, Kent won three competitions. The Benson and Hedges Cup, the John Player League and the end-of-season Fenner Trophy all found their way to the Kent trophy room. Denness himself did well as a batsman, scoring 1,165 runs at an average of 41.60. In 1974 Denness was heavily involved in the Test series and so, for the first time since 1963, he failed to pass a thousand runs in Championship games, though he did enjoy a successful benefit. The following season, he once again scored over a thousand runs: 1,088 at an average of 41.84.

In 1976 it was Denness who led the side to success in the Benson and Hedges Cup and John Player League, yet he later resigned the captaincy and joined Essex. In the semi-final of the Benson and Hedges Cup against Surrey at the Oval, Denness hit a superb century to lead Kent to victory. Throughout his last season with Kent he played some fine innings, hitting hundreds against Northamptonshire at Canterbury and Yorkshire at Scarborough.

As a fieldsman, Denness set a shining example by his athletic exploits in the covers, preferring to field there as, despite his quick reflexes, he often lost concentration if he fielded closer to the wicket!

Under his captaincy Kent won the Sunday League three times, the Benson and Hedges Cup twice and the Gillette Cup once. It was a blow to Kent when, in 1977, this outwardly tough but inwardly sensitive Scotsman left, to move to Essex.

Graham Dilley

Birthplace:	Dartford, Kent
Born:	18 May 1959
Died:	
Played:	1977-1986

Averages in all first-class Kent matches:

Matches	Innings	Not Outs	Runs	Highest Score	Average	100s
109	116	39	993	81	12.89	—

Runs	Wickets	Average	Best Analysis	5wI	10wM	Catches
7,146	257	27.80	6 for 57	10	1	51

Number of Test Appearances: 26

The circumstances of Graham Dilley's rise from a promising fast bowler to that of leading England's attack have been unusual to say the least.

He learned his cricket, initially, playing with his father and brother as a toddler on Dartford Heath. After progressing through various school teams he was, at the age of 15, given the opportunity of Saturday morning net practice with Kent. However, when he did leave school he had to take a job as a diamond setter in Hatton Garden. He soon gave up this job when he was offered the chance to play for the Kent Second XI in midweek games.

During the winter months he would build up his strength for the coming summer by carrying huge sheets of plasterboard for his uncle's partitioning firm. He would play for Kent Seconds in midweek and his club side, Dartford, at the weekends.

In 1977 his chance came and he made his first team debut against Cambridge University at Fenners. The following summer he made his Championship debut against Middlesex at Lord's, impressing straightaway with 5 for 32 in Middlesex's second innings. At the end of that season Dilley had taken 46 County Championship wickets; he also gained early international honours when he played for England against the West Indies in the Agatha Christie Under 19 Test series. His early performances had been enough to convince Mike Brearley and the Test selectors that he was a worthy choice to tour Australia in the winter of 1979-80. So, despite still being uncapped by Kent, he packed his bags for 'Down Under'.

He was selected to tour Australia on the basis that he was going to gain experience. But if Dilley thought his part in the trip would be fairly small, he was mistaken. He was selected for the first Test ahead of players like

Bob Willis who was struggling for fitness and form. Dilley had a very satisfactory Test debut, taking 3 for 97 from 36 overs and hitting 38 not out and 16 with the bat. Generally on that tour he bowled well, but often without stamina.

The following summer, when the West Indies were visiting, Dilley was surprisingly overlooked until the third Test at Old Trafford. His first Test wicket on English soil was Gordon Greenidge; representing England in three weather-interrupted Tests, he picked up 11 wickets at 16.63 runs apiece. Anybody watching Dilley bowl in that series must surely have noticed that he made one or two of the West Indies batsmen jump with his pace and bounce.

In 1980-81 Dilley toured the West Indies and although he only took 10 wickets in all of the four Tests at a rather expensive average of 45 runs, he impressed with his aggression and speed.

In that magnificent match at Headingly in the 1981 Ashes series, Dilley hit 56 runs, helping Man-of-the-Match Botham put on 117 for the eighth wicket. At the end of that series, Alan Knott suggested that Dilley try to add the outswinger to his armoury. Keith Fletcher, England's captain on the 1981-82 tour to India, insisted that Dilley be part of the trip. It was only a moderately successful trip for him, but by the end of the 1982 season he had bowled 466 overs in Championship games, taking 54 wickets – a struggle, but plenty of dedication by Dilley. During that summer he took 5 for 69 for the MCC against India at Lords's, but he didn't play at Test level that season and wasn't considered for the winter tour to Australia and New Zealand. So, instead he went to play for the Wanderers Club in Johannesburg.

In 1983 he started the season with a bang, uprooting Graham Gooch's off stump and taking 5 for 70 in a 6-wicket victory that was rain affected. Kent reached the Nat West Final against Somerset and although they lost, Dilley took 4 for 29.

He was chosen for the 1983-84 tour to Fiji, New Zealand and Pakistan, but injuries in the first leg of the trip were a great disappointment to him. In the first Test at Faisalabad he took 3 for 101 in 28 overs, though he had Pakistan's century maker, Salim Malik (116) 'out' twice by no-balls!

Dilley has performed that hat-trick on two occasions: against Surrey at the Oval in 1985, and at Chelmsford in the match against Essex a year later.

At the end of the 1986 season Kent revealed that Dilley had refused to sign a new two-year contract, but it also came to light that he had asked to be released some twelve months earlier. Dilley refused to re-sign for Kent, believing that the money side was less than he expected, though he had admitted that he had become slightly more mercenary! He felt that if Kent had made a reasonable gesture during his time in Australia he would have signed. On 1 January he became a free agent under TCCB rules. The Kent

Committee probably thought that Dilley would wait until 1990 and the chance of a benefit, but he left and joined Worcestershire.

At heart Dilley was still a Kent player, but he wasn't prepared to let loyalty stand in the way of financial security.

Edward Dillon

Birthplace:	Penge, London
Born:	15 February 1881
Died:	20 April 1941
Played:	1900-1913

Averages in all first-class Kent matches:

Matches	Innings	Not Outs	Runs	Highest Score	Average	100s
223	348	22	9,415	141	28.88	12

Runs	Wickets	Average	Best Analysis	5wI	10wM	Catches
1,321	27	48.92	3 for 20	—	—	195

Number of Test Appearances: 0

Edward Wentworth Dillon attended Rugby, where he achieved early fame in the game of cricket by topping the First XI batting averages in 1899 and 1900. In the latter of these two years he scored 620 runs at an average of 56.36, with a top score of 157. He also hit an unbeaten 110 when Marlborough were defeated by 9 wickets at Lord's, this score coming out of 190 runs, which were scored in two hours and within a quarter-of-an-hour of time. This was also the match when he took 6 for 84 with his slow left-hand bowling. He was described in Wisden as the best school batsman of the year, 'having also covered himself with glory for Kent'.

He made his debut for Kent in that year of 1900, averaging 36.50 from eight innings.

Dillon then went to Oxford University, where he got his Blue as a freshman. The match against Cambridge was drawn, but he did hit 143 against Somerset when Oxford were in a bad position. The following year, despite Dillon's scores of 85 and 59, Oxford were beaten by Cambridge. This in the main was due to Dillon's Kent colleague, S H Day, hitting 117 not out.

After being the leading batsman at Oxford in his second year there, Dillon went into business. However, he maintained his form and seldom disappointed with his batting when he returned from periods of very little practice to bolster the Kent batting. Whilst he was at Oxford he finished second in the Kent batting averages, to Jack Mason, his top score being 103 not out.

In 1902 he carried his bat for 38 when Kent were dismissed for 86 against Nottinghamshire at Gravesend. This was also the year that he toured the West Indies with B J T Bosanquet's side, following it in 1903 with a trip to America with the Kent side.

Ted Dillon was a left-handed batsman who believed in attack, with the off-drive being his favourite stroke. He used his long reach to the best advantage. He drove to the off with tremendous power and placed all his forcing shots with great skill.

In 1905 Dillon scored 1,310 runs at an average of 48.51. He also shared in a second wicket stand of 261 with Jim Seymour againat Somerset at Taunton.

In 1906 his batting average was 43.23, Dillon playing many of his better innings as an opener. It was Dillon who led the county to their Championship successes in 1909, 1910 and 1913. Jack Mason had resumed as captain for the last month of 1909 when Dillon had stopped playing for business reasons. This was often the case and it stopped him from completing a season's cricket.

Dillon led the side from 1909 to 1913, leading such players as the Day brothers, 'Punter' Humphreys, Colin Blythe, and Frank Woolley, Fred Huish, Arthur Fielder and D W Carr. Having said that, Dillon led the side shrewdly, Kent winning three out of their four Championships under his command.

Ted Dillon was a batsman capable of defending bravely when needed, but also good at going forward when the runs were needed. In 1913 at the Oval he scored 135 in a vain attempt to stop Surrey winning. He more or less finished his county career by leading Kent to the 1913 Championship. Yorkshire was certainly one county to suffer from Dillon's bat. In the 1910 fixture at Dewsbury Dillon slaughtered the White-Rose attack, hitting 138 as Kent won by 9 wickets. In the return at Maidstone, he hit a rapid 49, enabling Blythe and Woolley to dismiss the visitors, Kent winning by 178 runs.

Dillon was also a Rugby Union Internationalist. Whilst playing three-quarters for his club, Blackheath, he was capped against Ireland, Scotland and Wales in 1904 and then Wales again in 1905.

He died aged 61 in April 1941, a successful captain and believer in attacking cricket.

Alan Dixon

Birthplace:	Dartford, Kent
Born:	27 November 1933
Died:	
Played:	1950-1970

Averages in all first-class Kent matches:

Matches	Innings	Not Outs	Runs	Highest Score	Average	100s
378	576	71	9,561	125*	18.93	3

Runs	Wickets	Average	Best Analysis	5wI	10wM	Catches
23,869	929	25.69	8 for 61	46	10	155

Number of Test Appearances: 0

Alan Dixon attended Dartford Technical College as a boy, also attending Alf Gover's Cricket School, where he received his first coaching. He had trials with Kent at the ages of 14 and 15 and, following his third trial at Canterbury, he was offered a position on the Kent staff.

In 1950, at the age of only 16, he realised his early ambition to play for his native county. His debut was against Essex at Clacton, but unfortunately there was no fairy-tale ending. Kent were well beaten by 10 wickets and Dixon only contributed 3 runs with the bat and his bowling was expensive, over 9 runs per over. He soon realised that it was a big step up to the county game but it was a challenge and he accepted it.

It was for Alan Dixon a long road. For the majority of the 1950s he was involved in club cricket with Swanscombe and Greenhithe and later Dartford, occasionally being recalled by Kent for the odd game. He was in and out of the Kent First XI for quite a number of years, but by 1959 he had arrived.

His early promise was as a batsman. He thrilled the Kent crowds with his adventurous style of stroke playing.

In 1959 he passed the thousand-run mark for the first time, scoring 1,045 runs in the County Championship at an average of 23.22.

The following year he once again topped the thousand-run mark for the season, scoring 1,089 runs for an average of 31.11. He also began to bowl, both medium-pace using the seam or quickish off-breaks and finished second in the county averages. At the end of the season he was awarded his county cap – ten years after his debut!

In 1961 he passed a thousand runs for the third consecutive year, scoring 1,156 runs at an average of 25.13. Alan Dixon was now developing into a very useful all-rounder.

Three years later, in 1964, he had developed into a very capable stock bowler. His batting form wasn't as consistent, though he still produced useful and attractive innings. In 1964 he took 122 wickets in the County Championship at a cost of 23.89 runs each. He bowled more overs this season than any other Kent bowler. His best performances that summer included 12 for 49 against Essex at Blackheath, 8 for 61 against Northamptonshire and 8 for 73 against Lancashire. He continued to bowl well the following two seasons, passing the one-hundredth wicket mark on both occasions. 1965 saw him take 117 wickets at a cost of 24.58 runs apiece and then, in 1966, 115 wickets at 21.39 runs each.

By 1967 Alan Dixon had been appointed vice-captain to Colin Cowdrey. He was now a true professional, very rarely having a bad game. In fact, in the summer of 1967 he had two outstanding games. In the Gillette Cup game at the Oval against Surrey, this bespectacled dual-purpose bowler (though he bowled medium-pace on this occasion) destroyed the Surrey batting by taking 7 for 15. He took 7 of the first 8 wickets to fall. He was made Man of the Match for a performance that is still a Gillette Cup record. Also that summer the tourists were India; Kent beat them, due in the main to a century and 5 wickets from Alan Dixon. In total, he scored only three centuries, but his best scores always seemed to come when Kent were up against it. Like the true professional he was, he worked harder when the odds were against him. He was awarded a benefit in 1969, but at the end of the 1970 season he decided to retire to go into insurance full-time. In all first-class matches he scored 9,561 runs and took 929 wickets. His biggest regret was never being chosen to tour, though he must have enjoyed his parting shot from first-class cricket, hitting the last ball he faced onto the roof of the Mayor's tent at the St Lawrence Ground for a six!

Paul Downton

Birthplace:	Farnborough, Kent	
Born:	4 April 1957	
Died:		
Played:	1977-1979	

Averages in all first-class Kent matches:

Matches	Innings	Not Outs	Runs	Highest Score	Average	100s
45	45	10	396	31	11.31	—

Runs	Wickets	Average	Best Analysis	5wI	10wM	Caught	Stumped
—	—	—	—	—	—	97	2

Number of Test Appearances: 0 (30 with Middlesex)

Paul Rupert Downton is the son of George Downton, a club cricketer who played with Sevenoaks Vine and made several first-class appearances for Kent in the late 40s.

Paul was interested in the game of cricket from a very early age and played for his prep school side when only 9 years old. At that time he played as a batsman and a slow bowler. When he moved to Sevenoaks School he was still playing as an all-rounder when he first played for the under-13 team. However, within twelve months he was playing as a wicket-keeper, a position in which he was always interested. In these early years, Paul was helped greatly by two people in particular. The first was John Miles, an Australian who ran a coaching school in Melbourne with Frank 'Typhoon' Tyson. The other who played a leading role was Alan Hurd, a player with Cambridge University and Essex. He was Downton's cricket master and English tutor. At Sevenoaks Paul had six seasons in a side that was unbeaten for three years.

He played for his father's team at Sevenoaks, moving up through the Third and Second XIs before keeping wicket in the First XI. He eventually made his Kent Second XI debut at the age of only 16. He shared the wicket-keeping role in that one-day match against the Army. His first Second XI Championship game was in 1974 against Surrey at Dover. During that season and in 1975 he played in about half the Championship games for the Kent Second XI. The following year he accepted Kent's offer of a full-time contract. In 1975-76 Downton toured the West Indies with the England Young Cricketers.

He made his first-team debut the following summer against Surrey at Maidstone, marking his appearance with the brilliant stumping of Alan Butcher off Asif's bowling. Perhaps this one incident went a long way

towards Paul winning a surprise tour place. In Kent's first innings, Paul batted at number ten, making 31 not out. Paul kept wicket in six further first-team matches, collecting 22 victims.

Paul received help in those early years from Kent's wicket-keepers of the past. Alan Knott passed on a great deal of advice, as did Les Ames and 'Hopper' Levett. Downton had now moved from Sevenoaks School to Exeter University, where he was studying law. After twelve months he was given a year's absence from his studies. Even at this early stage Downton was beginning to feel frustrated as Knott's understudy, but his selection for the winter tour to Pakistan and New Zealand eased the situation. He profited from playing in the highest class of cricket and throughout that tour he kept wicket competently.

In 1979 he was awarded his county cap, but at the end of the season he was confronted with the fact that Kent had offered Knott a further contract, which he had accepted.

64

After great soul searching he decided to join Middlesex. He had already impressed ex-Middlesex and England wicket-keeper, John Murray, a Test selector when Downton was chosen for the 1977-78 tour. It must have been a very difficult decision for Downton to make, especially considering his popularity with team mates and supporters.

His loyalty to the county of his birth had to make way for his need to play first-class cricket on a regular basis rather than the need to play first-class cricket for Kent on a limited basis.

If Paul had stayed with the White Horse county, there is no doubt in my mind that he would have followed Knott in the long list of outstanding Kent wicket-keepers. As it is, he moved on to Middlesex, where he has kept wicket with great determination, and made thirty appearances for his country.

Alan Ealham

Birthplace:	Willesborough, Kent
Born:	30 August 1944
Died:	
Played:	1966-1982

Averages in all first-class Kent matches:

Matches	Innings	Not Outs	Runs	Highest Score	Average	100s
305	466	68	10,996	153	27.62	7

Runs	Wickets	Average	Best Analysis	5wI	10wM	Catches
189	3	63.00	1 for 1	—	—	175

Number of Test Appearances: 0

Alan George Ernest Ealham was born at Willesborough, near Ashford. At the age of 13 his father, who never doubted his son's cricketing ability, suggested that he move from the local Willesborough club to the more glamorous Ashford club. The standards were much higher here and the coaching under the Association of Kent Cricket Club's Scheme soon developed him enough for Kent's Les Ames to come and see him play.

Kent offered him terms but his father, quite sensibly, wouldn't let him join the staff until he'd completed his apprenticeship as a welder and panel beater. At the age of 17 he was established in the Kent Second XI, gaining much from Colin Page's direction. Ealham had built up a very good reputation with Ashford as a batsman, but in those days he could bowl as well.

At the age of 21 he made his First team debut for Kent against Somerset in June 1966. The Bath ground wasn't the ideal one on which to make your debut but Kent won and Ealham scored 37 and 57 not out. He played about half of the matches in that 1966 season.

Alan Ealham was one of the best outfielders in the country and early in his career, in 1967, he took a most memorable catch off the bat of Fred Trueman. Kent were bidding to wrest the Championship title away from Yorkshire. Alan Ealham was fielding as substitute in the deep during a tense moment in this important encounter at Canterbury. Fred Trueman hit the ball a tremendous distance and at great height, Ealham running at full speed round the boundary, taking a brilliant one-handed catch in front of the Frank Woolley stand. The Kent crowd went wild, but Trueman disputed the catch, needing several minutes of convincing that he was indeed out.

In 1967 again he played in about half the games, but was in Kent's side when they won the Gillette Cup against Somerset. The next three seasons weren't successful ones for Ealham but in 1970, in the match against Nottinghamshire at Folkestone, he hit 57 in a rapid century-partnership which started the dramatic turn-round that enabled Kent to win. Yet he had to wait until 1971 before he established himself in the Kent side at number four. The season before, Kent had won the County Championship, so the first match that year was the traditional one at Lord's against the MCC. Ealham made 20 not out in Kent's first innings. The following match, at Dartford against Leicestershire, he hit a hundred and went on to pass a thousand runs for the season for the first time. In the Championship he scored 1,363 runs at an average of 34.94. The following season, only a couple of seasons after being awarded his county cap, he lost his place in the Kent side until the first Test and considered leaving the county. Fortunately for Kent he stayed. He was a very compact batsman, more of a striker of the ball than a stroker.

Ealham was renown for his fielding. As early as 1966 he took five catches in one innings in the match against Gloucestershire at Folkestone. In 1973 in the televised John Player League fixture against Leicestershire, he caught Chris Balderstone in breathtaking fashion; it was a catch shown time and time again on television transmissions. Perhaps his proudest moment came when he was twelfth man for England in the Jubilee Test against Australia at Lord's. He held two catches and was complimented by all in the England ranks.

In 1976 he once again passed a thousand runs in Championship matches; Ealham scoring 1,105 runs at an average of 33.48, his highest score this season being 134 against Nottinghamshire at Trent Bridge.

In 1977, when Kent shared the County Championship, he scored 1,116 runs (average 39.85). Ealham could always force the pace and he showed this in Kent's Benson and Hedges quarter-final match with Sussex at

Canterbury. Sussex had scored 264 and it seemed enough. Ealham had other ideas; he coaxed Chris Cowdrey to his maiden century, but it was his controlled hitting of 94 not out that saw Kent home. Even though Ealham had a good season with the bat in 1977, he never reached three figures. His highest score that summer was 99 against Yorkshire at Folkestone.

In 1978 he was asked to take charge of the Kent side, a team full of talent. He had his doubts, but his philosophy of always having a go if the opportunity presents itself was a wise one. He kept harmony in the side, despite the outside problems, and under his sensible captaincy Kent won the Championship and the Benson and Hedges Trophy. In 1979 he helped Chris Tavare put on 251 for the fourth wicket against Worcestershire at Canterbury. Two years later, he retired from the first-class scene to run a garage business. Ealham always rose to a challenge and surely his limited-overs talents could have been utilised by the national side.

The story doesn't end there, because in 1988 he was asked to captain the Kent Second XI. His brief was to work closely alongside Chris Cowdrey; Kent hope that his belief in team discipline and good standards of behaviour off the field will go a long way to help their assault on the major competitions.

Ealham's long term ambition is to succeed Colin Page, Kent's director of coaching this year. Let us hope he is successful, for he has all the credentials to bring back the glory days for Kent.

Godfrey Evans

Birthplace:	Finchley, London
Born:	18 August 1925
Died:	
Played:	1939-1967

Averages in all first-class Kent matches:

Matches	Innings	Not Outs	Runs	Highest Score	Average	100s
258	451	15	9,325	144	21.38	4

Runs	Wickets	Average	Best Analysis	5wI	10wM	Caught	Stumped
215	2	107.50	2 for 50	—	—	451	103

Number of Test Appearances: 91

Godfrey Evans was educated at Kent College, where his love of cricket developed. He was taken on the Kent staff at the age of 16 as a hard-hitting batsman who could also keep wicket. In 1937 his interest in boxing led him to obtain a professional licence. He had three fights as a welterweight (winning the first two on knock-outs and the third on points). He broke his nose in his third fight and was given an ultimatum by the Kent Committee: Boxing or Cricket.

He made his Kent debut in 1939 against Derbyshire. Evans soon took his first victim, R H R Buckston, who edged the second ball of the second over bowled by Norman Harding. The catch was spectacularly taken down the leg-side – the first of many in that vein.

Along came the war, Evans having six years of easy runs whilst playing cricket for the Army. His form in the wartime matches at Lord's was outstanding as a wicket-keeper. As a batsman, the games may just have turned him into more of a wild hitter rather than a serious batsman.

When cricket resumed in 1946 he was awarded his county cap, soon establishing himself as a wicket-keeper in the highest Kentish traditions. It was no surprise when he was selected to go to Australia at the end of that season. Officially, he went on that tour as understudy to P A Gibb and so didn't play in the first Test. After the first Test Evans took over. He went on to play in 91 Test matches for England, claiming 219 victims – 173 caught and 46 stumped. Many of his victims were out to half-chances.

In 1947, in the match against Derbyshire at Canterbury, Evans claimed 8 victims: 5 caught and 3 stumped.

As a batsman in the Second XI at Kent in his early days, he showed that the ability was there. He had all the strokes but, in the main, he didn't take his batting seriously and would play to the crowd, they in return encouraging him to do so! Potentially though, he was a good batsman and he certainly showed this when batting at international level. Of his seven centuries, two were made in Tests.

There are two occasions of Evans's batting in Test matches that show his ability right across the spectrum. At Adelaide in 1947 he showed that he could defend with patience and resource. He supported Middlesex's Denis Compton for ninety minutes without scoring a single run.

At Lord's he failed by only two runs to score a hundred off the Indian attack before lunch. In the dressing room he shrugged off all sympathisers with a typical, 'Those sort of records are for the real batsmen, not for the likes of me.' At Old Trafford in 1950 he did get a hundred on the most difficult of pitches. In his 91 Tests, he scored 2,439 runs.

His best season for Kent with the bat was 1952, when, for the only time in his career, he topped the thousand-run mark. He scored 1,241 runs at an average of 28.86.

Godfrey Evans had all the qualities of a born wicket-keeper: a superb pair of hands, agility, balance, anticipation, and perhaps, most of all, vitality. He was a shrewd tactician, spotting weaknesses in a batsman and passing on the tips to the bowler. On the other hand, he was so enthusiastic that he would keep up a non-stop chatter of encouragement to his team-mates, both in the changing room and on the field of play. At his very best, Evans was capable of making catches and taking stumpings which no other man would have even considered chances. He was superb standing back, good near the stumps and possibly the fastest mover everywhere!

Like so many of the cricketing greats, he thrived on the big occasion. It is probably fair to say that he was normally a better wicket-keeper for his country than for his county. Having said that, if he was just half as good for Kent as he was for England, then he would still have been the best on the county circuit!

Evans was a born entertainer and so, possessing a flair for the spectacular, was a favourite worldwide with spectators. He could also dismiss instantly from his mind any simple mistake that he might make.

This is to say that he did have his off-days but on his day, and there were many of these, then perhaps he was the greatest of all.

In 1949, when the tourists were New Zealand, he claimed 9 wickets (8 caught, 1 stumped) in Kent's match with them at Canterbury.

In terms of Test cricket, there are three well documented instances of his heroics behind the wickets. In 1948, at Trent Bridge, Barnes edged Jim Laker on to Evans's right foot. It lobbed into the air behind him. Evans launched himself to bring off an unbelievable catch.

In 1950, at Brisbane, Loxton edged Freddie Brown to Evans but he couldn't hold it. The ball rebounded back towards the bowler but Evans hadn't finished. He dived full length down the wicket and got his glove under the ball before it hit the ground.

In the Melbourne Test of 1955 Evans dived to catch Keith Miller – a catch that players of both sides still rave about.

After making his Test debut in that 1946-47 tour to Australia, he was England's Number One for the next thirteen years. Only when his selection was no longer automatic did he decide to hang up his gloves. Though he retired officially in 1959, he was called back in 1967 when Alan Knott was on Test duty. He kept superbly, the large crowds witnessing Evans catch both Illingworth and Taylor.

For Kent, he scored 9,325 runs and claimed 554 victims. For England he scored 2,439 runs and claimed 219 victims. Whether he was batting or keeping wicket, there was never a dull moment when Godfrey Evans was around.

Arthur Fagg

Birthplace:	Chartham, Kent
Born:	18 June 1915
Died:	13 September 1977
Played:	1932-1957

Averages in all first-class Kent matches:

Matches	Innings	Not Outs	Runs	Highest Score	Average	100s
414	767	44	26,072	269*	36.06	55

Runs	Wickets	Average	Best Analysis	5wI	10wM	Catches
47	0	—	—	—	—	411 (plus 7 st)

Number of Test Appearances: 5

Arthur Edward Fagg was born at Chartham, near Canterbury, and attended Payne Smiths School, but his cricket was born of his own enthusiasm and not through the school. Arthur would play on the local recreation ground and park and at weekends would help Joe Murrin on the St Lawrence Ground. Joe took a keen interest in young Arthur and arranged for him to have a net trial. Unfortunately, too many shots were played on the leg-side and Kent turned him down. Later in the season, the Club and Ground team were a player short and Arthur was called into the side. He batted at number seven, where he scored over 50 and earned himself a three-month trial the next year. In 1932, at the age of 18, he made his county debut at Edgbaston against Warwickshire.

Within two years, he had scored his first hundred for the county and passed 1,000 runs for the season. In 1935, he totalled 1,835 runs with a batting average of 32.76. In the mid-thirties Herbert Sutcliffe, the Yorkshire batsman, was dropping out of Test cricket. England were looking for a new opening partnership. Fagg and Hutton were thought of as obvious candidates with Fagg, a year older than Hutton, considered the best of the two!

Fagg made his Test debut against India in 1936. He played in two Tests in that series, his top score being 39. He fared much better in the County Championship, scoring 1,858 runs with a top score of 257 against Hampshire at Southampton.

He was selected for the tour to Australia, led by Middlesex's Gubby Allen in 1936-37. He played in the first two Tests but, having contracted rheumatic fever, he was invalided home. The fever affected his heart and caused him to play no more cricket until 1938, missing the entire 1937 season.

The season of 1938 was a good one for Fagg. He scored 2,456 runs, including nine centuries. One feat that summer that is likely to remain unique was Fagg's performance in the match against Essex at Colchester. He scored 244 and 202 not out, all the more remarkable considering his two previous scores were 0 and 1. It is highly unlikely that batsmen today will face enough deliveries to match Fagg's feat. Despite his splendid season, Fagg was not considered for Tests until the final one and then, after picking him, he was one of those left out. He did play in one more Test match, against the West Indies in 1939.

During the war, because he was unfit for the Services, he served in the Auxiliary Fire Service, before moving to Cheltenham College. Here he mixed work in the agricultural department, where his knowledge of gardening and vegetable production was invaluable, with cricket coaching. When first-class cricket was resumed after the war in 1946 he felt doubtful as to whether he could stand the strain and so stayed at Cheltenham.

He didn't return to the post-war game until 1947, after which he scored plenty of runs for Kent. He was 32 at this time and, due to the fact that Hutton and Washbrook were set as England's openers, he didn't play Test cricket again.

Fagg, though, was a very good county batsman. He had a full range of strokes and was one of those players who are apt to score faster than the crowd realises. Unlike many Kent players, he was at his best against the faster bowlers and was an especially severe hooker on any ball pitched short.

After scoring 203 against Middlesex at Dover in 1948, he saved his other scores of over 200 for the Nottinghamshire attack. He hit 221 in 1951 and 269 not out in 1953, both at Trent Bridge. Fagg's runs came during a somewhat depressing period in Kent's history in the early 1950s until 1957.

The season following, he devoted himself to a scheme where he visited the Kent schools in an attempt to create enthusiasm for the game, while keeping a watch for any promising young cricketer. Unfortunately the scheme wasn't a success and so, in 1959, he was appointed to the umpires list.

Arthur Fagg was a man of principles. Whilst umpiring in the England v West Indies match at Edgbaston in 1973, he took exception to the West Indies' attitude when he gave Boycott not out, and declined to stand at the beginning of the third day's play. Alan Oakman, the Warwickshire coach and former first-class umpire, took his place but after one over Fagg, having made his point, resumed duty.

Arthur Fagg died at Tunbridge Wells in September 1977, aged 62. Although in a career spanning from 1932 to 1957 he scored 27,291 runs in all first-class matches at an average of 36.05 and with 58 hundreds, it cannot be said that he ever fulfilled expectations.

William Fairservice

Birthplace: Nunhead, London
Born: 16 May 1888
Died: 26 June 1971
Played: 1902-1921

Averages in all first-class Kent matches:

Matches	Innings	Not Outs	Runs	Highest Score	Average	100s
301	417	96	4,922	61*	15.33	—

Runs	Wickets	Average	Best Analysis	5wI	10wM	Catches
19,272	853	22.59	7 for 44	38	7	164

Number of Test Appearances: 0

William John Fairservice, like many other Kent greats, attended Tonbridge Nursery under the expert guidance of coach Captain McCanlis.

He was a professional off-break bowler of medium-pace, making his debut for the Kent First XI in 1902. Like all bowlers, except the really greatest, he required a little help from the wicket to be completely formidable. In 1903 he claimed his first victim in first-class cricket. This was no less a player than W G Grace, whom he bowled twice in a match with the MCC at Lord's.

However, in the main, up to the outbreak of war in 1914 Fairservice was the spare man of the Kent side. He was the man who was left out of the side when room had to be found for someone else. Even when he did get in the Kent side he very rarely got a chance to bowl on a turning wicket. Charlie Blythe and Frank Woolley gaining preference. Kent must have been a happy county in those days, with reserves like Fairservice in the wings. There is no doubt that in different circumstances he would have been an even greater bowler.

As a batsman he could play some good shots on the off-side and often made useful contributions coming in late in the order.

In 1919 in the match against the Australians at Canterbury, he gave wicket-keepr Jack Hubble great help in saving the game, whilst facing the pace of Gregory. Altogether in the first-class game he scored 4,922 runs at an average of 15.33.

After the war he commanded a regular place in the Kent line-up. In 1920 he reached the target of 100 wickets for the first time. He actually finished with 111 County Championship wickets at a cost of 17.46 runs each. I'm sure if he'd been with another county and not had players like

Blythe and Woolley to contend with, then he would have got his hundred wickets a season much earlier.

In 1920, in the match against Surrey at Blackheath, he showed what he could do when conditions were in his favour. He took 10 for 58 in this match, including the dismissal of Jack Hobbs (twice!). He dismissed Hobbs for 11 in the first innings and 0 in the second. He backed this up with match figures of 9 for 62 against Worcestershire at Tonbridge.

When the use of the new ball became firmly established, Fairservice would open the bowling instead of Blythe, except on a turning wicket. Even so, 1920 was the only season that he took over a hundred wickets in a season.

Altogether, he took 853 wickets at a cost of 22.59 runs apiece. A useful fielder, he picked up 164 catches.

After leaving Kent at the end of the 1921 season, he played Minor County cricket for a few years with Northumberland. He followed this with three coaching jobs at Tonbridge, Malvern and Lancing, before spending a few years as landlord of the 'White Horse' at Bridge.

After the Second World War he became scorer to the Kent Second XI, a position he held until he retired at the age of 77. When over 80 years old he still assisted his son, who played for Kent and was Sports Master at King's School, Canterbury, by bowling in the nets. He died in June 1971, the unluckiest of Kent bowlers.

Arthur Fielder

Birthplace:	Plaxtol, Kent
Born:	19 July 1877
Died:	30 August 1949
Played:	1900-1914

Averages in all first-class Kent matches:

Matches	Innings	Not Outs	Runs	Highest Score	Average	100s
253	329	154	2,000	112*	11.42	1

Runs	Wickets	Average	Best Analysis	5wI	10wM	Catches
24,014	1,150	20.88	9 for 108	88	25	106

Number of Test Appearances: 6

Arthur Fielder was born at Plaxtol near Tonbridge, his early enthusiasm for the game of cricket being fulfilled by engagements at both Canterbury and Tonbridge. He was eventually offered a place in the Kent First XI, as a replacement for Bill Bradley in 1903. It was a wettish summer, but he performed quite well, so much so that he was selected to tour Australia that autumn with Plum Warner's side. However, he didn't perform to his full capabilities and only played in two of the five Test matches.

It was Plum Warner, himself a notable player of fast bowling, who said that he found Fielder the most difficult of all fast bowlers. Fielder made the ball run away, bowling largely on the off-stump, for catches in the slips

A. FIELDER. (KENT)

Mockford
Tonbridge

or by the wicket-keeper. He could also pitch one on middle and leg to hit the off-stump and occasionally bowled one to make the ball come back. With the ball primarily swinging away, Fielder was dependent on having a strong back-up team. This he had; the brilliant Fed Huish behind the wickets and any combination of Ken Hutchings, Jack Mason, Jim Seymour and Frank Woolley in the slips.

When Kent won the County Championship in 1906 Arthur Fielder contributed greatly to their success. His great fast bowling was a decisive factor – taking 172 wickets at a cost of 20.55 runs apiece. This was also the year that he took all 10 wickets for 90 runs when representing the Players against the Gentlemen at Lord's. This distinction has not been achieved by any other player, before or since. Despite his magnificent performance, the Gentlemen won the game by 45 runs.

In 1907 he took 159 wickets at a cost of 16.60 runs each. During this season, in the game against Lancashire at Canterbury, he took what were to be his best bowling figures in the County Championship, 9 for 108. In fact, by the end of May he had taken 49 wickets in the County Championship at a cost of only 8.69 runs apiece.

He went to Australia again in 1907-08 under the leadership of Nottinghamshire's A O Jones. Fielder played in four Test matches, coming second in the Test match averages with 25 wickets at a cost of 25.08. His greatest moment came in the first innings of the first Test. Fielder took 6 for 82, his victims included Armstrong, Hill, Macartney, Noble and Trumper. Unfortunately he never represented England in a home Test series.

Arthur Fielder was never rated highly as a batsman, but in 1909 he hit his one and only century. He scored a chanceless unbeaten 112 against Worcestershire at Stourbridge, helping Frank Woolley to put on 235 for the tenth wicket. This is still a record in county cricket.

In 1911, he once again passed the hundred-wicket mark, taking 119 wickets at a cost of 20.98 each. Two years later, in 1913, he captured 113 wickets at a cost of 19.66 runs each.

When cricket was resumed after the war, Arthur Fielder was over 40 years of age and played no further part in Kent cricket. After his retirement from the first-class game he was coach at Rugby for a number of years.

A formidable opening bowler, he died in St Thomas's Hospital, London, in 1949, aged 71.

'Tich' Freeman

Birthplace: Lewisham, London
Born: 17 May 1888
Died: 28 January 1965
Played: 1914-1936

Averages in all first-class Kent matches:

Matches	Innings	Not Outs	Runs	Highest Score	Average	100s
506	630	170	4,257	66	9.25	—

Runs	Wickets	Average	Best Analysis	5wI	10wM	Catches
58,944	3,340	17.64	10 for 53	348	128	202

Number of Test Appearances: 12

There are not too many cricketers instantly recognisable by their nickname, but one is Alfred Percy Freeman, who was born in Lewisham on 17 May 1888 into a cricketing family. In his early days as a cricketer Freeman had been on the ground staff at Leyton when his uncle was groundsman. He played in several Club and Ground matches for Essex, but they didn't engage him! He was with the Upper Tooting Club from 1909-11, playing with some success as a leg-break and googly bowler. Kent asked him to join the staff at Tonbridge in 1912. During the 1912-13 seasons 'Tich', as he was to be known throughout the cricket world, was performing nobly in the Second XI. He was top of the bowling averages and also leading wicket-taker in Club and Ground matches.

In 1914 as a 'Young Player' Freeman took 135 wickets for Kent in representative matches, but more important than his performances in minor cricket was the fact that he played his first game for the Kent First XI. The game was against Oxford University at the Parks, Freeman going on to play in seven matches before the war came. He accomplished little, with the possible exception that he bowled Tom Hayward at the Oval.

In 1919 Freeman had to start all over again, but by the time the 1920 season was over he had taken his place among the best slow bowlers of the day.

'Tich' was only 5ft 2ins in height – he hurried back to the end of his run as if he couldn't wait to bowl the next ball. He relied mainly on a leg-break and a top-spinner which was difficult to spot – it was his most dangerous ball and provided him with many an lbw decision. He also possessed a much slower ball, cleverly flighted, often resulting in a skied catch or a stumping. In the main, it was the left-handers who were faced with the googly, though he would bowl it to the right-handers if necessary.

79

In 1920 he passed the hundred-wicket mark for the first time, taking 102 wickets at a cost of 16.88 runs apiece. It was a feat he was to achieve in greater terms each season until his retirement in 1936. His best performance in 1920 was his 9 for 87 against Sussex at Hastings, the Sussex captain declaring when the ninth wicket went down! At Canterbury in the match against Middlesex 'Tich' performed the first of his three hat-tricks.

In 1922, 'Tich' had his best season so far, taking 194 wickets. He took 17 of them in the match against Sussex at Hove, including 9 for 11 in the first innings as they were bowled out for just 47. In the return fixture he claimed another 12 victims to finish with 29 wickets for 138 runs in the two matches against Sussex, for an unbelievable average of 4.74. Wisden commented at the end of the season: '. . . at the top of his form, keeping a remarkable length to his leg-breaks and every now and then bowling genuine and well-disguised googlies. Seldom or never did he fail to take advantage of a treacherous wicket.'

In 1922-23, 'Tich' was selected to tour Australia and New Zealand with the MCC captained by Archie MacLaren, who was 51 years old and was to play his last first-class match on that tour. It was on this tour that Freeman was to take his second hat-trick at Adelaide in the match against South Australia.

'Tich' made the first of his twelve appearances for England on the 1924-25 tour. Though he did quite well in other matches, he only took eight wickets in the two Tests he played, at a cost of 57.37 runs each. As a batsman he was better than his figures suggest, scoring his maiden 50 in first-class cricket in his first Test on that tour. It was a very courageous innings, typical of 'Tich' Freeman. It was evident, on his return to England for the 1925 season, that he had enjoyed his batting in Australia. At Old Trafford he hit his maiden 50 in English first-class cricket, eventually being bowled by Ted McDonald for 66.

At the end of the 1925 season Kent made their customary tour of Scotland. A 12-a-side match was arranged with Berwickshire and District. 'Tich' didn't bowl in the first innings, but in the second, after George Collins had taken the first wicket, 'Tich' took the 10 remaining wickets for 34 runs in 12 overs. The top scorer for Berwickshire was Lord Dunglass, better known as Sir Alec Douglas-Home, who was lbw to 'Tich' for 21.

Freeman's most potent weapon was the top-spinner. In the first week of the August Canterbury week, 1927, Kent were entertaining Hampshire. Kent had batted supremely well for 407 and Freeman had destroyed Hampshire in their first innings, taking 6 for 38, as Hampshire crumbled to 81 all out. In their second innings the great Philip Mead hit a century and looked to have saved the game for his side. The last over began with Hampshire 9 wickets down; Mead had not faced a googly, the Kent players couldn't understand why. As Mead pushed forward to the first ball of the last over, it was the googly . . . too late, he was taken at slip by

A.E.FREEMAN.
KENT.

PHOTO
B.C.FLEMONS
TONBRIDGE.

81

Woolley and Kent had won by an innings. Freeman took 8 for 91 in the innings to give him match figures of 14 for 129.

His most successful summer was that of 1928, when his victims totalled 304 (including 246 in the County Championship). It was on 15 September when he became the first and surely the last bowler to take 300 wickets in a first-class season. For Freeman, 1928 was a season of continuous success – one could write a book alone on this one summer! Wisden stated that 'Kent owed most to Freeman, who putting a rare amount of spin on the ball and flighting it cleverly, bowled with so much skill that he went from one triumph to another.' Some of his better performances in the 1928 County Championship, included 13 for 168 against Northamptonshire and 12 for 199 against Hampshire, but the counties weren't the only sides to suffer at the hands of 'Tich'.

At Lord's on 23 June 1928 he made his home debut in a Test against the West Indies. It was an historic occasion as it was the first Test match ever given to the West Indies. Freeman's first wicket in Test cricket in England was Learie Constantine, who hit the first ball he faced from 'Tich' into the air where Larwood took a simple catch. Freeman went on to be the outstanding bowler of the three Test series, taking 22 wickets at 13.72 runs apiece. When the West Indies side played Kent at Canterbury they had no trouble in beating the White Horse county, though Freeman bowled superbly to take 9 for 104.

In 1929 'Tich' took all 10 wickets in an innings against Lancashire for 131 runs at Maidstone. He was to accomplish the feat a further two times in his career. In 1930 he took 10 for 53 against Essex at Southend and then 10 for 79 the following year at Old Trafford with Lancashire once again the county to suffer. In 1929 he produced his best figures in a Test match, taking 12 for 171 against South Africa at Old Trafford, going on to top the bowling averages for the season.

In 1930 'Tich' took 104 wickets from 21 May to 20 June, perhaps the only time 100 wickets have been taken in a one-month period. In the month of June itself 'Tich' took 91 wickets.

By the end of the 1931 season 'Tich' had claimed four great records: he had taken over 200 wickets for the fourth consecutive season; he had established a new record aggregate of 1,122 wickets in four seasons; he had passed Colin Blythe's record of 2,231 wickets for Kent; also he became the first bowler to take all 10 wickets three times in first-class cricket – this he did for the third summer in succession.

In 1932 he took 17 wickets in a match for the second time. Against Warwickshire at Folkestone, he had match figures of 17 for 92 (8 for 31 and 9 for 61). He was the leading wicket-taker in the country that season, showing his importance to the Kent side in that he took 209 County Championship wickets, the same total that the other 13 bowlers amassed between them!

In 1934 he performed the third and final hat-trick of his career, against Surrey at Blackheath.

In the eight seasons between 1928-35 he took 2,090 wickets at an average of 17.85 runs apiece.

The end of his career was a little sad. In 1936 he took 79 wickets in the first two months and then only 29 in the next two. He could no longer stand the strain of a full season. It was suggested that he play only in selected matches with rest periods in between, but he rejected the proposal. The Kent Committee terminated his engagement with the county.

Following his retirement from first-class cricket, he spent a couple of years at the Gorway Ground playing for Walsall in the Birmingham and District League. He then retired to a house near Maidstone, which he called 'Dunbolyn'.

'Tich' Freeman died on 28 January 1965, three months short of his 77th birthday, the greatest wicket-taker county cricket has ever known.

Dave Halfyard

Birthplace:	Winchmore Hill, London
Born:	3 April 1931
Died:	
Played:	1956-1964

Averages in all first-class Kent matches:

Matches	Innings	Not Outs	Runs	Highest Score	Average	100s
185	274	31	2,538	79	10.44	—

Runs	Wickets	Average	Best Analysis	5wI	10wM	Catches
18.822	769	24.47	9 for 39	49	13	88

Number of Test Appearances: 0

Dave Halfyard was born in Winchmore Hill, London, and was on the staff at the Oval for three years before joining Kent. At Surrey he was a tearaway pace bowler, unable to force his way into the First XI.

He played his first game for Kent in 1956 and, though he took wickets, he was quite expensive over the season as a whole.

The following season he took 117 County Championship wickets at a cost of 21.38 runs each. In the match against Worcestershire at Folkestone he took 7 for 45 in the first innings and 6 for 49 in the second. In this match

D.J. HALFYARD
KENT.

84

he performed the hat-trick for the first time. Later that season he claimed what were to be the best figures of his career. The opponents were Glamorgan, the venue Neath, as Halfyard ripped open the Welsh sides batting, taking 9 for 39.

Dave Halfyard was a super stock bowler. He was a captain's dream; all he had to do was to put him on one end and leave him to do the rest. Halfyard liked nothing better than bowling. He had the perfect build for hours of toil, but he certainly didn't bowl on automatic pilot! Halfyard possessed many subtleties of cut and changes of pace.

In 1958, on a wet wicket at Hastings, he took 8 for 49 to help shoot out Sussex. In the same season at Gillingham he took 5 wickets in each innings to help defeat Leicestershire. He took 5 for 21 in the first innings, including the second hat-trick of his career, and 5 for 81 in the second. In all County Championship matches that summer he took 135 wickets at a cost of 19.91 runs each. In 1959 he took 15 wickets in the match against Worcestershire at Maidstone, 6 for 56 in the first innings and 9 for 61 in the second. He ended the season with 125 wickets at a cost of 24.98 runs apiece.

In 1960 Worcestershire were again the county to suffer at the hands of Halfyard. He took 4 for 7 and 5 for 20, as the Tunbridge Wells crowd thrilled to his outstanding bowling. That season saw him take 123 wickets at 22.11 runs each. The following summer saw him take over 100 wickets for the fifth consecutive season, 112 wickets at 29.26 runs – it was to be the last time. There was no doubt about it, he was one of the mainstays of the Kent bowling attack.

On 10 August 1962 Dave Halfyard was injured in a car crash on the Banwell to Weston-super-Mare road. He suffered a broken right leg and lacerations of the face. In 1963 he was still recovering and unable to play a game. He took gret pains to get fully fit but, after playing in only two games in 1964, he was thanked for his services, given a testimonial and allowed to go. In these two games he had taken only one wicket at a cost of 179 runs and it seemed that his career was over. He looked to have lost both his pace and his enthusiasm for the game. As a batsman he was a big-hitter in the tail-end of the Kent batting line-up. He also possessed a safe pair of hands, but it was as a fast-medium stock bowler that he made his name at Kent. He ended his Kent career with 769 wickets at a cost of 24.47 runs each.

In 1967 Halfyard was a first-class umpire, but all the time keeping himself fit with a hope of returning to the first-class game. In 1968 he joined Nottinghamshire, becoming a regular and valuable member of the Midlands side.

He later played for Cornwall, turning in some memorable performances, but for Kent he was a player of great determination, liking nothing better than when he was bowling.

William Hardinge

Birthplace:	Greenwich, London	
Born:	25 February 1886	
Died:	8 May 1965	
Played:	1902-1933	

Averages in all first-class Kent matches:

Matches	Innings	Not Outs	Runs	Highest Score	Average	100s
606	990	98	32,549	263*	36.48	73

Runs	Wickets	Average	Best Analysis	5wI	10wM	Catches
9,773	370	26.41	7 for 64	8	1	286

Number of Test Appearances: 1

Harold Thomas William Hardinge, or 'Wally' as he was known, made his debut for the Kent First XI in 1902. He went on to play for Kent for almost a quarter of a century, although it was 1908 before he really made his mark.

In 1908 he scored 1,341 runs at an average of 33.52, his best performance being at Leyton in the match against Essex, when he scored 153 in the first innings and 126 in the second. He was to perform this feat on a further three occasions.

Hardinge was also one of a small number of men who played internationally at both cricket and soccer. His Test debut came much later, but in 1910 he played soccer against Scotland at Hampden Park. He was a centre forward and played professionally for Arsenal and Sheffield United.

In 1911 he scored 1,146 runs at an average of 33.70. In the match against Hampshire he scored 175 in the first innings, following it up with 109 in the second. He also carried his bat, scoring 123 out of Kent's total of 203, in the match against Essex at Tonbridge. This was also the year that he made his debut for the Gentlemen in the fixtures against the Players. He scored over a 1,000 runs in both 1912 and 1914, but 1913 was without doubt his best season before the war. He scored some 2,018 runs at an average of 42.93. He scored four centuries in successive innings. The first came against Leicestershire when he hit an unbeaten 154. He followed that up with centuries in both innings against Hampshire at Dover, 117 and 105 not out. The fourth hundred came against Northamptonshire, when he scored 107.

Wally Hardinge was a very good player against fast-medium and medium bowlers and especially good on a turning wicket against the slow spinners. He would play very close to his legs, a compact, solid batsman whose footwork was immaculate. He possessed a wide array of strokes, all of them beautifully executed. His favourite shots were the cut and the off-drive but he could also hit well to leg and his role in the Kent batting line-up was often as the sheet-anchor, his run-rate seemingly slower in comparison to his team-mates.

As one would expect in the outfield from a soccer international, he was fast and possessed a safe pair of hands. He certainly saved Kent hundreds of runs on the boundary. As a bowler, he wasn't required in the the strong pre-First World War sides, but after the war he proved invaluable in breaking stubborn partnerships. He was a slow left-hand bowler who, in the main, kept to a good length, occasionally pitching the ball up in an attempt to lure the batsman into a false shot. He was a far shrewder bowler than the batsmen gave him credit for. Perhaps for other counties he would have been a regular bowler, but he still took 370 wickets for Kent.

In 1919 he carried his bat on two occasions, the most notable being in the match against Essex at Colchester, Hardinge scoring 172 out of Kent's total of 339. In 1920 he scored 1,216 runs at an average of 30.40, but it was the following year when he was selected for England.

He had made his highest score, 127 at the Oval for the Gentlemen against the Players, in what was his fourth match in the six he played. At Blackheath against Surrey, he scored 207 and 102 not out to register for a fourth time. He also carried his bat for 118 out of Kent's total of 196 in the match against the MCC at Lord's. His one and only Test came against Australia that year at Headingley, when Jack Hobbs had to withdraw on the opening day because of appendicitis. Despite his good performances that season, his selection was a little bit of a surprise, because he was never really sound against very fast bowling and Gregory and McDonald comprised Australia's opening attack! Hardinge scored 25 and 5.

The following season he scored 2,068 runs at an average of 57.44. He carried his bat for 249 runs against Leicestershire and shared in a second wicket partnership of 307 with Jim Seymour against Worcestershire at Kidderminster. He continued to top the thousand-run mark for the next three seasons. Then in 1926 he helped set the Kent record for the fourth wicket partnership, putting on 297 with Percy Chapman against Hampshire at Southampton. It was the season he scored 2,234 runs at an average of 47.53.

In 1928 Hardinge hit the highest score of his career, 263 not out against Gloucestershire, following it with another double century, 205 against Warwickshire at Tunbridge Wells. Altogether that season he scored 2,446 runs at an average of 59.65. In 1929 he achieved 6 for 9 as a bowler in 11.5

overs against Warwickshire. He hit 75 hundreds in his career and totalled some 33,519 in all first-class matches.

For many years he was on the business staff of John Wisden and Co Ltd. After his retirement he had several coaching appointments, later working for the Cement Marketing Board.

Wally Hardinge died at Cambridge in May 1965 at the age of 79, second only to Frank Woolley in the total number of runs scored by an individual for Kent.

W. HARDINGE.(KENT.)

Lord Harris

Birthplace:	St Annes, Trinidad	
Born:	3 February 1851	
Died:	24 March 1932	
Played:	1870-1911	

Averages in all first-class Kent matches:

Matches	Innings	Not Outs	Runs	Highest Score	Average	100s
157	278	17	7,842	176	30.04	10

Runs	Wickets	Average	Best Analysis	5wI	10wM	Catches
1,523	64	23.79	5 for 57	1	—	155

Number of Test Appearances: 4

To give him his full title, he was George Robert Canning, the fourth Baron Harris of Seringapatam and Mysore, and of Belmont, Kent, GCIE, GCSI, CB.

He was born on 3 February 1851 in Trinidad, where his father was Governor.

From 1868 until 1870 he played in the XI at Eton, captaining the side in his last year when Harrow were defeated. As a schoolboy he was coached by R A H Mitchell, his progress developing steadily rather than meteorically.

Living at the family home, Belmont, he was soon involved in Kent cricket, being on the preliminary committee when Kent County Cricket Club was reformed in December 1870. The previous August he had made his debut for Kent against the MCC at Canterbury, not performing to his full capabilities. In May 1871, however, he hit a superb 107 as a late replacement for the MCC against Oxford University. It was this innings that won him a place in the Oxford side and won him his Blue that year. Apart from the solitary exception of 1873, when he was injured, he won his Blue at Oxford each year until 1874. In 1874 he was captain and headed the batting averages with 23.20 and led Oxford to victory over rivals Cambridge.

It took him a few years to establish himself in the Kent side and, with his appearances sparse while at University, he did in 1872 tour Canada with R A Fitzgerald's team. That winter his father died and he succeeded to the title.

In 1875 he was appointed Kent's president, captain and honorary secretary! He more or less ruled the county club in some capacity or other for almost the next six decades. He was also heavily involved with the

MCC. He was a Trustee of the club for ten years, its Treasurer for sixteen years and its President in 1895.

When Lord Harris took charge the fortunes of Kent were low, but gradually his dedication encouraged the best amateurs to join him and a professional nucleus. It was certainly an uphill struggle, though his batting held the team together on many occasions. In his 157 matches he top-scored in 68 innings.

He took a team to Australia in 1878-79, where he scored more runs than his colleagues in the only representative match at Melbourne, which was lost. He scored 289 runs on the trip, with an average of 32.11. Lord Harris possessed great courage. In the match at Sydney an angry mob rushed on to the field, protesting at an umpiring decision. Harris moved forward to shield one of the umpires and was hit by a stick for his trouble.

Following this episode, there was something of a crisis in Anglo-Australian cricketing relations. However, it was Lord Harris himself who put an end to this unrest by inviting the Australians to tour England. He captained the English side to victory in what was the very first Test match held at home.

In 1882 at Canterbury, in the match against Middlesex, he scored 72 and 101, but it wasn't enough to save Kent from defeat. In the same season he hit his highest career score, 176 at Gravesend against Sussex. In 1883 he hit a faultless 118 against Lancashire at Old Trafford. In 1884 Harris hit hundreds against Derbyshire, Sussex and Hampshire. This was the season when Kent were the only county to beat the Australians. It was a real team effort, though Lord Harris led by example, scoring 60 and taking four catches.

Lord Harris also held two Government posts before becoming Governor of Bombay. He did much there to popularise the game and, in fact, organised the first English tour to India, the party being led by Yorkshire's Lord Hawke. He fought in the Boer War with the Imperial Yeomanry and was an important person in the City of London. It would be hard to find a more representative figure in the heyday of the Empire than Lord Harris. Whilst he was in India, he was instrumental in launching Ranjitsinhji. However, when it came to the suggestion that on the basis of his Cambridge and Sussex connections he should play for England, Harris strongly disagreed!

On his return from India, he made only a few appearances in 1896, hitting 119 in his second game of the season against Somerset at Taunton. His last appearance for Kent was against All India in 1911, when he scored 36.

Lord Harris was a stickler for principles. When referring to the Laws of the game, he insisted that 'Laws were made to be kept, Rules made to be broken.' It was this strict attitude to the Laws that made him a fierce opponent of any opposing bowler who was suspected of throwing.

Lancashire's Crossland and Nash were just two suspected and so Lord Harris ordered the Kent Committee to cancel all fixtures against the Red-Rose county until both bowlers were no longer in the side. Another example was when Harris discovered that the young Walter Hammond was playing for Gloucestershire, when he had been born and bred in Kent. Harris sent an edict from the MCC. This put an end to young Hammond's livelihood until he fulfilled certain requirements!

Lord Harris lived for cricket and played his last match at the age of 79!

He was a formidable autocrat, fair-minded and not used to having his authority questioned, but he was sympathetic to those whose views he held in respect. A man of great character, he died at Belmont, Kent, on 24 March 1932.

Alec Hearne

Birthplace:	Ealing, London
Born:	22 July 1863
Died:	16 May 1952
Played:	1884-1906

Averages in all first-class Kent matches:

Matches	Innings	Not Outs	Runs	Highest Score	Average	100s
403	687	63	13,598	162*	21.79	11

Runs	Wickets	Average	Best Analysis	5wI	10wM	Catches
23,023	1,018	19.96	8 for 15	46	9	352

Number of Test Appearances: 1

Alec Hearne was born in Ealing in July 1863, qualifying for Kent from the fact that his father, 'old George Hearne', was groundsman at Catford Bridge, where Kent played their home games in 1875.

When Alec made his debut for Kent in 1884 he was a clever leg-break bowler who had an excellent command of length, flight and spin. During the season Kent were the only county side to beat the Australians led by Murdoch. Hearne took 7 for 66 (including 5 for 36 in the first innings) to make his mark.

In 1885, at Bramall Lane in the match against Yorkshire, he took 5 for 13 in the first innings and 8 for 35 in the second. He was a constant thorn in the side of the northern county. The following season when Australia returned, he took 4 for 37 at Canterbury, Kent winning by 10 wickets. In 1888, he performed the hat-trick whilst representing the MCC against Yorkshire at Lord's. His second hat-trick was against Gloucestershire at Clifton in 1900.

About this time he reverted to bowling off-breaks, as the strain on his elbow, through the bowling of leg-breaks, was beginning to take its toll. However, he was still bowling with considerable success.

He produced some remarkable bowling figures. In 1902 against Somerset, he took 4 for 0 at Taunton; 5 for 13 against Warwickshire at Maidstone; 5 for 15 against Hampshire at Tonbridge; 8 for 36 against Middlesex at Lord's; and 4 for 10 against Gloucestershire at Tonbridge. In 1903 he bowled unchanged with Colin Blythe to take 7 for 61 against Surrey at the Oval. His career best-bowling anaylis, 8 for 15, was against Gloucestershire at Tonbridge. Still his greatest hope was to become a good batsman. He had started as a number ten, but worked so hard at this side of his game that for quite a few years he was Kent's opening batsman.

The Australians found Alec Hearne a stubborn obstacle whenever they met him. For Kent he scored 24 and 35 in 1890 when the Australians were beaten at Canterbury. Three years later he scored 20 and 39 and took 8 wickets as the Australians were beaten again. This season saw him represent the South against the Australians at the Oval, when he scored 120 and took 17 wickets in the match. In 1899, at the Crystal Palace, he scored the highest score of his career, 168 for W G Grace's XI against the beleaguered Australians.

He was a very neat batsman, strong on the back foot, with the cut his favourite shot. He was also a quick and accurate hooker, especially on slow wickets.

In 1891-92 he toured South Africa with W W Read's team and made his only Test appearance at Cape Town, scoring 9, holding one catch, but not bowling. In this match his brother George and cousin John Thomas played for England, whilst his other brother Frank played for South Africa.

In 1895 he scored 1,076 runs at an average of 28.31; his top score of 155 coming in the match against Gloucestershire at Gravesend. This was the match in which W G Grace was on the field while every ball was bowled. In 1898 he scored 1,171 runs at an average of 36.59. The following year against Nottinghamshire at Trent Bridge, he helped Jack Mason put on 321 in an unbeaten third-wicket stand to establish the Kent record for this wicket. During this stand he scored his highest score in county cricket, 162 not out.

In 1901 he scored 1,022 runs at an average of 28.38. It was the third time he'd passed the thousand-run mark. In 1906, Hearne's last season in the Kent First XI saw him go out of the game in a flourish. His last six innings saw him score 291 runs, his highest score being an undefeated 154 against Worcestershire at New Road.

He was awarded two benefits, the first for Kent against Lancashire in 1898 and then in 1913 for the MCC in the shape of the Middlesex v Hampshire game.

On his retirement from the game he was coach at the Tonbridge Nursery. In 1925 he replaced his cousin, Walter, who had died, as county scorer. He kept the position until 1939, despite being crippled by rheumatism.

He died in May 1952, aged 88, a modest man but an excellent judge of cricket.

George Hearne

Birthplace: Ealing, London
Born: 7 July 1856
Died: 13 February 1932
Played: 1875-1895

Averages in all first-class Kent matches:

Matches	Innings	Not Outs	Runs	Highest Score	Average	100s
252	444	44	7,148	126	17.87	4

Runs	Wickets	Average	Best Analysis	5wI	10wM	Catches
9,393	569	16.50	8 for 21	35	10	175

Number of Test Appearances: 1

George Gibbons Hearne was born in Ealing and, like his younger brother Alec, he gained his qualification for Kent through his father being in charge of the ground at Catford Bridge, where Kent played all thier home games in 1875.

He made his debut for the Kent First XI in 1875, the first year of Lord Harris's captaincy. It was Lord Harris who spotted George Hearne and signed him up for Kent. Alec and Frank followed, and then two cousins; Kent's gain was Middlesex's loss. There is no doubt that Lord Harris's statement that in his first year he had found a gold mine was an understatement!

In the main, George Hearne was a bowler, left-hand round arm and fast-medium in pace. His stock ball was one that broke to off, giving many chances at slip, where C A Absalom missed little.

In his first season he took 8 for 46 against Lancashire at Old Trafford, including the hat-trick.

In 1877 George Hearne became the first man for Kent to take 100 wickets in a season, the actual figures being 105 wickets at 11.76 runs apiece. In the 1870s Hearne produced some outstanding bowling feats. Hampshire suffered twice at the hands of Hearne. He took 4 for 9 at Winchester and 13 for 75 at Southampton. He took 14 for 130 against Derbyshire at Derby and 8 for 53 against Lancashire at Canterbury. At Lord's he took 14 for 45 against the MCC. In 1877 and 1878 his efforts resulted in him taking 201 wickets at a cost of around 12 runs apiece. Altogether in his career he took 569 wickets at 16.50 runs each.

Like his brother Alec, he later developed into quite a capable left-handed batsman. He spent the last thirteen years of his career as a sound

consistent performer. Lord Harris wrote that his innings would have been even longer if his captain hadn't run him out so often!

His most successful season with the bat was 1886, when he fell just short of the thousand-run mark in the County Championship. He scored 987 runs for Kent that year, with an average of 41 runs. Altogether that season, he scored 1,125 runs in all first-class matches. In the match against Middlesex at Gravesend he scored 126, when George partnered his brother Frank in a stand of 226 runs. Against Yorkshire at Canterbury he scored 117, when he and Cecil Wilson put on 215 runs together.

In 1889 he scored 103 against Sussex at Gravesend, whilst sharing in a stand of 249 runs with Frank Marchant. At the end of the 1889 season Kent entertained Nottinghamshire at Beckenham. Nottinghamshire were favourites to win and thus carry off the County Championship, but in their second innings they were dismissed for 35 on what was a shocking wicket. Kent, set 52 to win, struggling to 25 for 6. Hearne entered the fray, batting for over a hundred minutes to score 14 not out and thus ensure a victory for Kent by 4 wickets. This result meant that the 1889 Championship was tied by Lancashire, Nottinghamshire and Surrey.

Hearne's one and only Test appearance came in the same match at Cape Town, in which his brother Alec also made his only appearance. Unfortunately, George failed to score and didn't have the opportunity to bowl. At the end of his first season for Kent, he was engaged at 'Prince's' and in 1877 started a liaison with the MCC which continued for many years.

George Hearne died in February 1932 at the age of 75, the first to die of that successful Kent side of 1884 which defeated the Australians.

Jack Hubble

Birthplace:	Wateringbury, Kent
Born:	10 February 1881
Died:	26 February 1965
Played:	1904-1929

Averages in all first-class Kent matches:

Matches	Innings	Not Outs	Runs	Highest Score	Average	100s
343	496	61	10,229	189	23.51	5

Runs	Wickets	Average	Best Analysis	5wI	10wM	Catches	Stumped
1	0	—	—	—	—	411	217

Number of Test Appearances: 0

John Charlton Hubble was born at Wateringbury and, like many other Kent cricketers, he attended the Tonbridge Nursery and was coached by the great Captain McCanlis.

He made his Kent debut in 1904 and although he was a very accomplished wicket-keeper he had to concentrate on his batting up to the war, as Fred Huish was behind the wickets.

98

In his first season he played for Kent in the match against Yorkshire at Harrogate. It was a match that was declared void due to the wicket being tampered with. At the end of the first day holes had appeared, but by the start of the second morning they had been filled in. There was a biggish crowd on the ground, so the game continued for their benefit, but the result didn't count towards the Championship. This was probably a big disappointment to Yorkshire's quickie, Schofield Haigh who, trying his hand at slow leg-breaks, picked up a hat-trick.

As a batsman, Hubble scored five centuries in his career, his highest being 189, made in less than three hours against Sussex at Tunbridge Wells in 1911.

The following season, in that remarkable game with Leicestershire, Hubble showed his fighting spirit. On a treacherous wicket Leicestershire were dismissed for only 25, with Colin Blythe taking 7 for 9. Kent too were in trouble, as Leicestershire's King took 8 for 26 but Jack Hubble, batting at number six, hit a forceful 46 out of 54 to see Kent to 110. It was the only type of innings that really had a chance of success on that wicket.

Hubble was particularly good at playing on the off-side and was often at his best, unlike some other players of his time, against fast bowling. His best season with the bat was 1914, when he scored 1,212 runs at an average of 33.66.

In 1919 Hubble replaced Fred Huish behind the wickets. Huish was a wicket-keeper well above the average. During that first season after the war Kent entertained the Australians at Canterbury. Kent were 165 for 7 when Hubble and Fairservice came together. Hubble showed his fondness for fast bowling, as he hit Australia's Gregory all round the St Lawrence Ground in making 71 not out. It must be said that he had great help from Fairservice and this helped Kent save the game.

In 1921 Hubble represented the MCC against the Australian's at Lord's. Few MCC batsmen could stand up to the pace of Gregory and McDonald, but Hubble showed his value with knocks of 42 and 25.

As a wicket-keeper, Hubble was not in the same league as Huish or Ames, but he was a most reliable county wicket-keeper.

In 1923, in the match against Gloucestershire at Cheltenham, he gave his best performance as a wicket-keeper. He claimed 10 victims (9 caught, 1 stumped) in the match; 6 victims were captured in the first innings and 4 in the second. In 1925 against Leicestershire he had 8 victims (6 caught, 2 stumped) and 8 victims (2 caught, 6 stumped) the following season in the match with Gloucestershire at Gravesend. This year was his most successful when he claimed 78 victims (44 caught, 34 stumped).

His first-class career with Kent ended in 1929. He scored 10,229 runs and captured 628 victims. Afterwards he continued to play and umpire for the MCC and run his own sports business.

He died in February 1965 at the age of 84, a great servant of Kent cricket.

Fred Huish

Birthplace: Clapham, London
Born: 15 November 1869
Died: 16 March 1957
Played: 1895-1914

Averages in all first-class Kent matches:

Matches	Innings	Not Outs	Runs	Highest Score	Average	100s
469	686	122	7,247	93	12.84	—

Runs	Wickets	Average	Best Analysis	5wI	10wM	Catches	Stumped
87	0	—	—	—	—	901	352

Number of Test Appearances: 0

Frederick Henry Huish was born at Clapham; a Surrey man who played for Kent. He learned his craft in his early days from Harry Wood, the Surrey wicket-keeper who was Kentish by birth.

He made his first-class debut in 1895, Kent having found themselves a reliable wicket-keeper, much to the relief of the White-Horse county bowlers!

Unfortunately, Huish was a contemporary of Warwickshire's Dick Lilley who was a better batsman, and so, despite his obvious international class, Huish never represented his country. He was one of the most able and least demonstrative wicket-keepers of his generation. In 1899, Huish assisted in the taking of 77 wickets in a season, 73 caught and 4 stumped; his best performance being the eight catches he took against Nottinghamshire at Trent Bridge.

Huish showed his abilities, albeit in lucky fashion, in Kent's match against the Australians at Canterbury in 1902. He was stood back to Bill Bradley when Australia's R A Duff played the ball a few yards behind the wicket and his partner set off for a run. To get to the ball, Huish had to move quite a way and, realising that he wouldn't have time to gather it before the batsman got home, he tried to kick the ball on to the wickets at his end. Huish had put so much power into his kick that the ball missed the nearest set of stumps, but went on and hit the wicket at the other end, Duff being run out by a yard!

Although Huish never represented England, in 1902 he made his one and only appearance for the Players against the Gentlemen at Lord's.

In 1905 he once again claimed 77 victims (54 caught, 23 stumped); his best performance being against Gloucestershire at Catford, when he

claimed 8 victims (7 caught, 1 stumped). Huish's skill in taking the slow bowling was a vital factor in Kent's great championship years.

In 1908 he assisted in the taking of 81 wickets, his best performance coming at Taunton, when he claimed six catches and two stumpings in the match.

Huish was among the few to assist in the taking of 100 wickets in a season. He achieved this performance on two occasions. In 1911 he became the first wicket-keeper to reach 100 victims, 62 caught and 39 stumped in his final total of 101. He claimed 8 victims (4 caught, 4 stumped) in the match against Northamptonshire, but his greatest triumph came in the match against Surrey at the Oval. The occasion was Herbert Strudwick's benefit match. Fred Huish stumped 9 and caught one. Stumped nine! If you were to look through a season's averages, there wouldn't be too many present-day wicket-keepers with that as their season's total!

In 1913 he raised his tally to 102 victims (70 caught, 32 stumped). There were three occasions during this season when Huish claimed 8 victims in a match. The sides to suffer at Huish's hands were Leicestershire, Middlesex and Lord Londesborough's XI at Scarborough. Huish was now 43 yeas old and had gone a long way in helping Kent win their fourth County Championship title.

On the whole, Huish wasn't successful as a batsman. His best year was 1906, when he scored 562 runs with a top score of 93 against Somerset at Gravesend. Yet nothing shows more clearly how highly Huish was rated by the Kent Committee. Jack Hubble had been playing as a batsman in the side for a number of years, but Huish was never left out of the Kent side. In fact, Huish was quite a useful man to have in any tail, constantly scoring thirties and forties – though I doubt whether any county side would have selected him for his batting alone.

On becoming Kent's senior professional, Huish was reputed to exercise remarkable control over his playing colleagues. The story goes that, unless he appealed, no other professional dared to ask for a catch at the wicket!

In his later life, he was for many years Secretary of the Sundridge Golf Club. He died at Northiam, Sussex, at the age of 87, the first in a line of exceptional Kent wicket-keepers.

Edward Humphreys

Birthplace:	Ditton, Kent
Born:	24 August 1881
Died:	6 November 1949
Played:	1899-1920

Averages in all first-class Kent matches:

Matches	Innings	Not Outs	Runs	Highest Score	Average	100s
366	590	44	15,308	208	28.03	19

Runs	Wickets	Average	Best Analysis	5wI	10wM	Catches
8,122	306	26.54	7 for 33	5	—	212

Number of Test Appearances: 0

Edward Humphreys, or 'Punter' as he became known, arrived at Tonbridge with his pads strapped around his bat, ready to play in a trial game; he was just 16 years of age. When he came on to bowl, he bowled a no-ball and was immediately sent from the field by Lord Harris. Humphreys thought that was the end of his hopes of playing for Kent. However, as Lord Harris explained to Humphreys, 'I did that for your good, whilst a fast-bowler can be excused an occasional no-ball, with a slow bowler it is more carelessness.' It was one of the best lessons a young cricketer could have, and Humphreys certainly learnt from it.

In 1899, at the age of 17, he made his first appearance for the county, as a slow left-arm bowler. But it wasn't long before he gained greater recognition as a right-hand opening batsman. He was quick on his feet to slow bowling, showing particular skill to the turning ball, but he wasn't as adept against quicker bowling.

In 1904 Humphreys scored 1,524 runs at an average of 36.28. In 1906 he showed his skill with the ball, taking 7 for 33 against Middlesex in their second innings in the match at Tonbridge. This was the year of Kent's first County Championship success and his bowling performance in this match went a long way in helping Kent avoid defeat.

In fact, 'Punter' Humphreys retained his place in the Kent line-up throughout the successful years of 1906-1913, when they won the County Championship on four occasions.

In 1908 he helped A P Day put on 248 in what is still a Kent record for the seventh wicket in the match at Taunton against Somerset. The following year, Humphreys scored 1,390 runs at an average of 39.71, including hitting the highest score of his career: 208 against Gloucestershire at Catford.

In 1910 he totalled 1,618 runs at an average of 36.77, including another double hundred: 200 not out, made at Tunbridge Wells against Lancashire. During this game he shared with A P Day (again!) a stand of 254 for the fifth wicket. In 1911 he scored 1,773 runs in County Championship games at an average of 42.21.

In 1912 he represented the Players at Lord's and wasn't far from being selected for the full England side. In 1912-13 he went to the West Indies as a member of the MCC team, captained by A F Somerset, and enjoyed a successful tour, scoring 461 runs (average 40.07) and taking 40 wickets at a cost of 16.75 runs apiece.

In 1913 he scored 1,587 runs at an average of 33.06, following it in 1914 with 1,355 runs at an average of 30.11.

In his playing career he played under five Kent captains, J R Mason, C J Burnup, C H B Marsham, E W Dillon and Lionel Troughton. Throughout his career, which spanned from 1899 to 1920, he scored 15,308 runs and took 306 wickets for Kent in first-class games. He also earned recognition for his superb fielding at either mid-on or short-leg. In the war he served with the Navy and was present at the raid on Zeebrugge.

During his playing days he went to Jamaica on five occasions to impart his knowledge to the young players out there – West Indian cricket owed him a great debt! Before this he had coached in New Zealand. After finishing first-class cricket 'Punter' Humphreys became coach at Uppingham School, where he was instrumental in the development of Percy Chapman and Gerry Chalk. He still had four years of his contract to run at Uppingham, when he was asked by Lord Harris to return to Kent as a chief coach. There is no doubting the fact that Edward Humphreys was a great coach. He never made the mistake of trying to teach too much in one net. He would always concentrate on ensuring that one stroke was played correctly. 'Punter' saw the rise of fellow-Kent greats, such as Arthur Fagg, Doug Wright and Godfrey Evans.

He was still coaching at the Nursery to within a year of his death. He died at his home in Maidstone in November 1949, aged 68.

Kenneth Hutchings

Birthplace:	Southborough, Kent
Born:	7 December 1882
Died:	3 September 1916
Played:	1902-1912

Averages in all first-class Kent matches:

Matches	Innings	Not Outs	Runs	Highest Score	Average	100s
163	238	12	7,977	176	35.29	19

Runs	Wickets	Average	Best Analysis	5wI	10wM	Catches
493	15	32.86	4 for 73	—	—	141

Number of Test Appearances: 7

Kenneth Hutchings was a true man of Kent. He was born in 1882 at Southborough, near Tunbridge Wells, and attended Tonbridge School. He had a great career at Tonbridge, being in the School XI for five years, heading the batting averages for the last three seasons. He hit 205 against West Kent and took hundreds off the Band of Brothers, Old Cliftonians, and Free Foresters twice.

He made his debut for Kent in 1902 at the age of 19. It was the following season when he first gave evidence of his ability in County cricket. He hit 106 against Somerset at Taunton.

Hutchings produced little until 1906, a year that will never be forgotten in Kent cricket. He was the most brilliant of batsmen that season, making his runs quickly and attractively. He didn't make his first appearance that season until 18 June when, as a comparatively unknown player, he started with 125 and 97 not out against Middlesex and from then until the end of the season he could do nothing wrong. It was in the Middlesex game that Hutchings received excellent support from Fred Huish who, despite suffering from lumbago and requiring a runner, managed to survive the final twelve minutes or so to save the game.

The following game was at Sheffield against Yorkshire, the then county champions. Despite being dropped twice early in his innings, he went on to score 131, this against the likes of Wilfred Rhodes, George Hirst and Schofield Haigh. It was said that in this game, even George Hirst, the most fearless of fieldsmen at mid-off, went back several yards for him, so terrific being the force of Hutchings's hitting. His next hundred was his highest career score of 176, made in three hours at Canterbury against Lancashire. His final century that season came at Bournemouth against Hampshire. He hit 124, reaching his century in an hour. He hit 1,454 runs at an average of 60.68 that season.

In 1907 he hit another four 100s. One was at Tonbridge against Hampshire, another at Canterbury against Lancashire (again!) and two in the same match against Worcestershire, where he'd returned after injury.

At the end of that season he went off with A O Jones's team to tour 'Down Under'. He didn't meet with the success expected of him; his only knock of any consequence was at Melbourne in the second Test, where he played a very fine innings of 126 (106 in boundaries). It was the only Test match that the English team won. On his return to the county scene in 1908, he hit tons against Derbyshire and Northamptonshire but the high spot was an innings of 120 in 100 minutes at Scarborough, when representing the Gentlemen against the Players.

The following year saw him score three more centuries, including one in fifty minutes at Catford against Gloucestershire. In 1910 he notched 1,461 runs; it was to be his last really impressive season. He scored five centuries, one for the Gentlemen and four for Kent. All of his hundreds had been made by the first week in July. There is no doubt about it, Hutchings was a fierce driver and certainly didn't believe in hanging around at the wicket. He hit 104 in 100 minutes at Northampton; 109 in 100 minutes at Tonbridge against Leicestershire; 122 in two hours at Derby; and 144 at Hastings.

In 1911 he didn't reach 1,000 runs and averaged 29.31, yet his only hundred was a typical effort, 103 not out in 100 minutes against Hampshire at Canterbury.

In 1912 he struggled to score 178 runs in ten innings and dropped out of the Kent side.

Hutchings was very strong in the wrists and forearms and was a tremendous driver of the ball. He was also equally good off the back-foot, being able to play the ball at the last moment. When he was in form, he was almost impossible to keep quiet. Hutchings was also one of the greatest of all fieldsmen, whether it be in the slips or on the boundary; the power of his throwing, which was entirely achieved by the flick of the wrist, is legendary.

Two years into the First World War Lieutenant Kenneth Lotherington Hutchings of the 4th Battalion The King's Liverpool Regiment was killed in battle. He was just two months short of his 34th birthday.

Hutchings was perhaps the most illustrious cricketer killed in the 1914-18 War, a dashing attacking batsman who was greatly mourned by Kent and cricket lovers in general.

Asif Iqbal

Birthplace:	Hyderabad, India
Born:	6 June 1943
Died:	
Played:	1968-1982

Averages in all first-class Kent matches:

Matches	Innings	Not Outs	Runs	Highest Score	Average	100s
243	399	42	13,231	171	37.06	26

Runs	Wickets	Average	Best Analysis	5wI	10wM	Catches
2,096	73	28.71	4 for 11	—	—	168

Number of Test Appearances: 58

Asif Iqbal was born into a cricketing family, no doubt inheriting much of his cricket from his father who played for Hyderabad, but died when Asif was only six months old. But where he lacked any parental guidance, he was well advised by his four uncles, all of whom were first-class cricketers. One of these was Ghulam Ahmed, the Indian off-break Test bowler. Such was their guidance that by 9 years of age he was in his school team.

Asif was told that he had plenty of talent and that one day he would become a good cricketer. Asif wanted to be a cricketer who enjoyed himself and as a youngster he would always hit the ball as hard as he could and bowl as fast as he could!

At the age of 17 he played in the Ranji Trophy for Hyderabad. In 1961, when Pakistan toured India, he represented the South Zone against them and took 6 wickets in the match. Also this year, he played against Ted Dexter's MCC side. Around this time most of his family, being Muslims, had emigrated to Pakistan and Asif later joined them.

In Pakistan Asif was considered more of a bowler, whereas in Hyderabad he had been thought of as a batsman. Through College and University, where he graduated in Economics and History, his reputation as an opening bowler and hard-hitting middle-order batsman was spreading.

In 1963 the Pakistan Eaglets, comprising of promising youngsters and a fair number of Test players, left for a short tour of England. The party included Hanif Mohammed and his younger brothers Mushtaq and Sadiq. Intikhab Alam, Majid Khan and, of course, Asif Iqbal. He spent the tour batting mostly at number eight, where he averaged 29 in eight innings. As a bowler, he took 19 first-class wickets at an average of 14.73. The amount

of movement that he could get in the air and off the wicket in English conditions was an exciting prospect for him.

In his first Test for Pakistan against Australia in 1964-65 at Karachi, he batted at number ten in the first innings and scored 41. In the second, he was moved to number three and scored 36. He also opened the bowling, picking up a couple of wickets. On his first major tour to Australia in 1965 he was the leading wicket-taker in the Test matches and headed the first-class bowling averages for the tour.

When Pakistan played at Wellington in the first Test against New Zealand there were the first signs of Asif's batting beginning to emerge. Pakistan were left with 259 to make to win the game, but started disastrously, their score being 19 for 5. Asif, batting at number eight, followed his first innings score of 30 with a match-saving 52 not out. Also during this series of three Tests, he took 18 wickets, including 5 for 48 and 7 for 33 at Wellington.

At the beginning of 1967 Asif was made captain of the side to face an under-25 team representing the MCC. The MCC manager was Les Ames, who immediately recognised Asif's leadership qualities. In the second of their encounters Asif hit his maiden first-class hundred to help save the game. This innings assured that Asif would make the trip to Engand.

In his first appearance against Kent he found that Les Ames hadn't forgotten him, nor had Colin Cowdrey who sounded Asif out about the possibilities of him joining Kent. In that 1967 Test series Asif was first noticed by the English public. In Pakistan's second innings in the third Test at the Oval, on the last day, they looked like losing by an innings, as they stood at 65 for 8. Asif hit 146 in three hours, the highest score by a number nine batsman in a Test match. In doing so, he became the hero that the Pakistanis in the crowd had hoped for. After off-driving Ken Higgs for 4 to bring up his maiden century, his countrymen raised him shoulder high. Even though England only needed 32 to win, it was Asif who made them fight all the way, dismissing Cowdrey and Close cheaply before they reached the total needed.

Asif joined Kent in 1968, bringing with him an uninhibited brand of cricket. He was a batsman of quality, a bowler who could cut or swing the ball, and a fielder with superb reflexes. In his first season he scored 1,236 runs at an average of 28.74.

In 1969, during Canterbury week, Asif came in with the Kent score on 89 for 4, trying to draw the game with Leicestershire, as they were 146 behind and there were still two hours to play. In fifty-one minutes, Asif hit 86 out of 92, playing a wide varity of strokes, on one of the wettest wickets that Canterbury had known.

In 1970 Asif batted to the peak of his power, scoring 1,379 runs (average 39.40). Perhaps the highlight of this year was on the last afternoon of the match against Gloucestershire at Cheltenham. Requiring 340 to win, Asif hit Allen, Mortimore and Bissex to all part of the ground, as he scored 109 – all this on a broken wicket! During the following season a game against a touring side was played at Gravesend, where Asif scored 50 for Pakistan in dismal conditions. This was also the season when he hit 91, that nearly brought Kent victory against Lancashire in the Gillette Cup Final. Asif was a sad man as he headed back to the pavilion, not because he'd missed his century, but because he felt he'd let his team-mates down.

Asif scored a thousand runs or more for Kent in the County Championship on six occasions, his best average of 48.53 coming in 1975, though 1970 was the year when he scored most runs in the Championship. He was awarded a well-deserved benefit in 1981, and also captained the side in 1977 and 1981-82 with great inspiration.

Perhaps his best season was the busy one of 1976-77 when Asif hit four centuries in three different series. Against New Zealand he scored 166, helping Javed Miandad set a fifth wicket record of 281. In Australia he averaged 78.25, scoring 313 runs, including centuries at Adelaide (152 not out) and Sydney (120), following it with 135 against the West Indies at Kingston, Jamaica. In all, he played in 58 Tests for Pakistan, scoring 3,575 runs at an average of 38.85, including eleven hundreds.

It was Asif who used the Packer affair in a positive way to get better money for all Pakistan's cricketers.

Asif retired from the first-class game in 1982. He will always be remembered by Kent followers as a constant and thrilling match-winner.

Graham Johnson

Birthplace:	Beckenham, Kent
Born:	8 November 1946
Died:	
Played:	1965-1985

Averages in all first-class Kent matches:

Matches	Innings	Not Outs	Runs	Highest Score	Average	100s
376	582	73	12,549	168	24.65	11

Runs	Wickets	Average	Best Analysis	5wI	10wM	Catches
17,058	555	30.73	7 for 76	22	3	271

Number of Test Appearances: 0

When Graham Johnson joined the Kent staff it was primarily as an off-spin bowler, but he developed into a batsman who also bowled.

He made his debut for Kent in 1965. At the time, Kent had an experienced batting side and Johnson was unsure as to whether he would make a career in cricket. He decided to take a degree at the London School of Economics to enable him to get a decent job if his cricket was a failure.

111

Beginning as an off-spinner, he lost his rhythm for a time; also as Underwood and the Kent seamers were bowling well, his chances were rather limited.

In 1969 Johnson showed a lot of promise as a batsman. He had the ability to push the ball on his legs wide of mid-on for 4 and endless time to play all shots.

In 1970 he played a significant role in Kent's Championship success. He played in twenty-five matches, scoring 927 runs at an average of 23.76. He was soon being hailed as an outstanding prospect in terms of both Kent and English cricket – a player with infallible signs of class! He hit a superb 116 against Sussex at Tunbridge Wells, and 108 against Leicestershire at Folkestone with devastating stroke-play, but it was the match against Surrey at Blackheath that Kent supporters will remember best. He took 12 for 151 in what was a match-winning performance. Surrey, needing 263 to win, required 12 runs to win from two balls. Graham Johnson tossed up a slow inviting half-volley to Surrey's England off-spinner Pat Pocock. He drove it high over mid-off, the ball seeming to be heading for a certain 6, but Asif raced along the boundary and took the most unbelievable of catches – Kent had won by 12 runs. Johnson improved so much that season that he became a regular member of the Kent side even when Test players like Knott, Cowdrey, Denness, Luckhurst and Underwood returned.

Whilst Underwood was away on Test-match duty Johnson had the opportunity to bowl. Whilst he very rarely ran through a side, he performed with great consistency, adding variety to an all-seam attack. He also had the knack of picking up wickets at crucial times and so, as the 1970s wore on, he became an essential part of the Kent bowling line-up.

In 1972 Johnson won the Man-of-the-Match award in the Gillette Cup match against Gloucestershire. The St Lawrence Ground had thousands of gallons of water pumped off it. Opening the innings, Johnson hit a magnificent 65, as Kent triumphed by 33 runs. This season was the start of his opening partnership with Luckhurst, Johnson batting with both power and style.

In 1973 Johnson passed the thousand runs in a season for the first time. In Championship matches he scored 1,362 runs at an average of 32.42. He followed this a year later with 1,005 runs at an average of 30.45, one of his best innings that season being his 158 made against Warwickshire at Canterbury. Johnson played an innings of pure quality, driving off the back and front foot as Brown and Willis tried everything they could to dislodge him. He also helped Brian Luckhurst to put on 256 for the first wicket against Derbyshire – it was the second highest first wicket stand for Kent.

In 1975 Johnson scored 1,366 runs in the County Championship (average 37.94) – it was the most runs scored for Kent that summer.

112

Johnson was also a magnificent slip fieldsman, with a beautiful pair of hands. In 1976 he held four catches for Kent in the Benson and Hedges Cup Final against Worcestershire at Lord's. He also shares with Alan Ealham the most catches, 68 for Kent in the Sunday League competition.

In 1977, the year Kent shared the Championship title with Middlesex, it was rather a disappointing season for Johnson. He required a cartilage operation and missed seven consecutive matches. He attempted to return much too early (due to his great enthusiasm) and didn't produced his best. When he was fit again he wasn't restored to his role of opening batsman, except for one-day games.

The 1979 Wisden commented on the difficulty of opening the batting one day and batting at number seven the next, but Wisden also added that 'Johnson made it pay off with distinct success.' Openers have come and gone for Kent, but Graham Johnson stayed, making valuable scores in the middle and lower order. Many Kent supporters thought that he'd found his real niche in the game.

In 1978 he scored 664 runs (average 26.56) and took 54 wickets at a cost of 18.94 runs apiece. Those figures should have found him a spot as an all-rounder in the England line-up, but they didn't. Perhaps Graham Johnson has just been in the wrong place at the wrong time.

Graham Johnson has many fine qualities, including his great ability as a coach and his willingness to pass on his knowledge to others. When Mike Denness departed at the end of the 1976 season Johnson was overlooked for the captaincy – it came as a great surprise to many. He went on to play for Kent until 1985 under various captains, his great adaptability in changing circumstances serving him well.

In his twenty years with Kent he scored 12,549 runs at an average of 24.65 and a highest score of 168; he also took 555 wickets at 30.73, with his best figures being 7 for 76.

But Graham Johnson was one of many very good county cricketers whose cricket statistics do not do justice to their many talents. He sacrificed his personal aims and ambitions to ensure Kent's success, remaining an integral part of the county side for twenty years.

Alan Knott

Birthplace:	Belvedere, Kent
Born:	9 April 1946
Died:	
Played:	1964-1985

Averages in all first-class Kent matches:

Matches	Innings	Not Outs	Runs	Highest Score	Average	100s
349	505	94	11,339	144	27.58	9

Runs	Wickets	Average	Best Analysis	5wI	10wM	Catches	Stumped
13	1	13.00	1 for 5	—	—	746	85

Number of Test Appearances: 95

In 1962 Alan Knott couldn't make up his mind whether to turn to cricket or, although he was due to leave the Northumberland Heath Secondary Modern, to try for extra 'O' Levels at school and thus enter College.

His father, who was a wicket-keeper with Belvedere, persuaded him to play cricket rather than stay on at school. Alan had already played representative cricket at school level for North-West Kent, South of England and England. Just before he turned professional, Kent suggested that he play for Blackheath, the best side in the area. During the summer of 1961-62 he played as a semi-professional with Kent. When he made his debut for the County Second XI, he didn't keep wicket, he played as a spinner!

He 1964 he kept wicket regularly in the Second XI, making his First team debut in June of that year against Cambridge University, captained by Mike Brearley at Folkestone. He took three catches and made the winning hit and stayed in the side to play Leicestershire next match.

He was capped by Kent the following year when he was elected the Best Young Cricketer of the Year. He claimed 81 victims this year (72 caught, 9 stumped). In 1966 he assisted in the dismissal of 80 batsmen (72 caught, 8 stumped), his most notable performances coming against Middlesex at Gravesend, and against Northamptonshire at Maidstone when he dismissed six batsmen in an innings on both occasions.

He made his England debut in 1967 against Pakistan at Trent Bridge. He was just 21 years old and he took seven catches, each one different. At the Oval, he had five catches and a stumping. It was a great start to his international career. On the county scene, he claimed 85 dismissals (78 caught, 7 stumped) – his highest in a season. His best performance behind

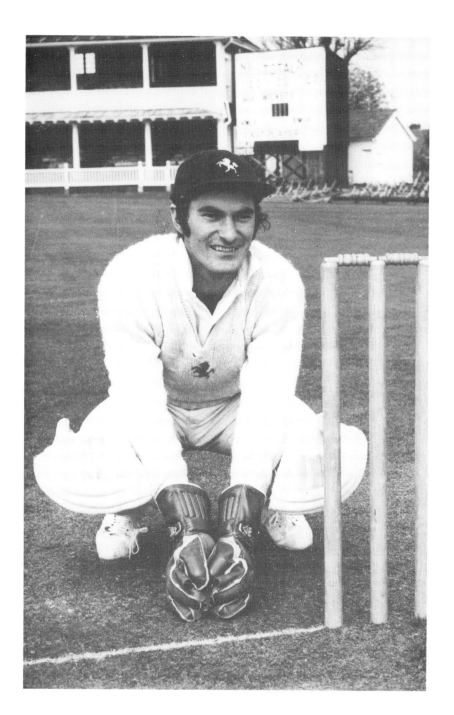

the wicket came against Leicestershire at Folkestone, when he held six catches in one innings.

At international level Knott gained a regular place as England's wicket-keeper in the fourth Test on the MCC tour of the West Indies in 1967-68. When they played at Georgetown, Knott saved the game, thus enabling England to win the series. In the last Test, England needed to bat all day or score 308 to win the game. They started disastrously and were soon 41 for 5, with Boycott, Edrich, Graveney, Barrington and D'Oliveira back in the pavilion. Knott, in only his fourth Test, joined his Kent colleague and England captain Colin Cowdrey, to add 127 for the sixth wicket on a wearing pitch. Cowdrey eventually fell for 82, but Knott was left undefeated on 69, after receiving valuable assistance from Snow, Lock, Pocock and Jeff Jones, who lasted out the final over.

In 1972 he scored a century in each innings of the match against Surrey at Blackheath, both of them unbeaten. He scored 127 not out in the first innings and 118 not out in the second. On the international scene, England had been given the run around by the Australians (nothing's changed!) and Bob Massie in particular. Massie had demolished England's batting at Lord's, but in the last Test at the Oval, Knott gained his revenge. He scored an exhilirating 92, thrashing Massie to all parts of the ground in the process.

He toured India on two occasions, getting the better of the Indian spinners by moving his feet to the pitch of the ball and hitting it over the top.

In 1973 Knott was as inspiring as ever behind the stumps, his best performance coming against Worcestershire at Dartford, when he once again dismissed six batsmen in an innings. He also achieved a batting average of 60 in only 11 first-class matches. In 1974 he took the Man-of-the-Match award in the Gillette Cup Final against Lancashire on the strength of his continued superb form behind the wicket.

On the tour of Australia in 1974-75, his batting was brilliant against the searing pace of Lillee and Thomson. In fact, he was England's second highest scorer. He had been robbed of a maiden Test century in Karachi in 1968 when rioting brought the match to an end when he was 96 not out. But he finally got his hundred against Pakistan at Edgbaston in 1971.

He learned much of his wicket-keeping from Les Ames, 'Hopper' Levett and Godfrey Evans. Apart from Derek Underwood, with whom Knotty quickly formed a deadly alliance, he didn't have too much spin to contend with in his vintage years, as his figures suggest with his stumping total. Knotty is probably best remembered by his superb acrobatic catches in 'no man's land' between him and first slip or else wide down the leg-side.

In a typical day behind the wicket he would go through his routine of callisthenics. Knotty's shirt collar was always turned up to keep the sun off his neck and his sleeves rolled down to protect his elbows when he dived.

In 1977 he set his record for the most dismissals in a match. This came at Maidstone in the match against Leicestershire, when he caught nine batsmen. After playing in the Centenary Test at Melbourne he became one of the first recruits to Kerry Packer's World Series Cricket. At the time he had played in 89 Tests. He went on to play in six further Tests, with only Australia's Rod Marsh bettering his 269 Test victims. He scored 4,389 runs for England at an average of 32.75. He scored five hundreds and thirty fifties, most of them coming when England were in dire straits. He was also the first England wicket-keeper after Ames to score a century in an England v Australia Test match.

In 1982 he helped Chris Tavare put on 256 in an unfinished sixth wicket partnership against Essex at Chelmsford. At the end of the 1985 season he decided to retire and is now an important member of the BBC Cricket Commentary Team.

For me, Alan Knott is the finest wicket-keeper since the Second World War, but I'm sure he would have been a great wicket-keeper in any cricketing period.

Stuart Leary

Birthplace:	Cape Town, South Africa
Born:	30 April 1933
Died:	23 August 1988
Played:	1951-1971

Averages in all first-class Kent matches:

Matches	Innings	Not Outs	Runs	Highest Score	Average	100s
381	617	92	16,169	158	30.79	18

Runs	Wickets	Average	Best Analysis	5wI	10wM	Catches
4,714	140	33.67	5 for 22	2	—	362

Number of Test Appearances: 0

Stuart Edward Leary was born in Cape Town, South Africa, in 1933. He attended Greenpoint High School where he gained a big sporting reputation. He was a capable fly-half at Rugby Union, and school cricket captain, but he showed more promise as a soccer player. He was spotted playing soccer for Clyde (Cape Town) by Jimmy Seed, the Charlton Athletic manager.

Leary arrived in England in 1949 with his friend Eddie Firmani. By 1952 Stuart Leary was a regular in the Charlton Athletic first-team, playing as a deep lying centre-forward. He had superb control and vision, creating goals both for himself and Firmani that saw Charlton shoot to fifth place in the 1954 First Division Championship. Leary scored 20 goals a season on a regular basis and his total of 170 plus league goals for Charlton is still a club record.

In his early days at the Valley, he mentioned to Jimmy Seed that he enjoyed playing cricket. He went to Seed's home town of Whitburn and the Durham League side soon offered him terms. Kent, to their credit stepped in and Leary joined the county staff in 1951. But his development was delayed due to his commitment on the soccer field and he had to serve two years' National Service in the RAF.

He was on the edge of the side for quite a few years, but by 1957 he had secured a regular place and was awarded his county cap. This was the first time he passed a thousand runs in a season, scoring 1,231 runs at an average of 36.20 runs.

Leary usually batted at number five, and was at his best in a crisis. His favourite shot was a variation of the push, prod and dab, though he was also a master of the sweep. He was quick on his feet, thus enabling him to steer the ball for ones and twos, to the annoyance of the opposition. His unorthodox approach to batting sometimes offended the purists and, because of his reputation as a slow scorer, he was once left out of a one-day match in 1969. He returned to hit three sixes in the next match. In 1970 he won the country's top six hit competition!

Leary topped 1,000 runs a season on nine occasions, his best season being 1961, when he scored 1,440 runs. It must also be remembered that until he gave up playing soccer in 1964, he was never available after Canterbury week.

The highest score of his career was 158 made against Northamptonshire, in which he shared in a third wicket stand of 283 with R C Wilson. In all first-class cricket he scored 16,517 runs at an average of 30.79, including eighteen centuries.

Leary was also a respected leg-break and googly bowler. He took 140 wickets at a cost of 33.67 runs each. As a fielder he was one of the best in the game. His razor-sharp reflexes brought him 362 catches, many at short leg. In 1958, at Fenners in Kent's game against Cambridge University, he equalled the Kent record by taking six catches in one innings.

In 1967 he enjoyed what was then a record benefit return, £9,100. It was also the last time he passed 1,000 runs, scoring 1,042 runs at an average of 30.64. His top score this season, 125, was also made against Northamptonshire at Gravesend.

Leary was a great humourist and mimic, always ready for a joke both on and off the field.

He had the distinction of leading the side several times towards the end of his last season in 1971.

He was a brilliant all-round sportsman, playing 381 first-class matches for Kent and 470 Football League matches for Charlton Athletic and Queens Park Rangers. He did gain an Under-23 cap for England, but was later judged ineligible due to his South African origin – this must have perplexed him, especially as he'd done two years' National Service with the RAF. Leary was an integral and very popular member of the successful Kent side.

After the 1971 season he returned home to South Africa, where he took up various coaching appointments, including a post at the University of Cape Town. He also gained a good reputation coaching black children at the Dominican School for the Deaf in Cape Town. He eventually became Director for Coaching for the Western Province Cricket Union and Manager of the Western Province Currie Cup team.

He never returned to England, for he loved his native South Africa. He was found dead on his beloved Table Mountain some four days after his car had been found abandoned. It was an untimely death and a sad end for a man who brought much happiness to all who knew him.

Howard Levett

Birthplace:	Goudhurst, Kent	
Born:	25 January 1908	
Died:		
Played:	1930-1947	

Averages in all first-class Kent matches:

Matches	Innings	Not Outs	Runs	Highest Score	Average	100s
142	214	44	2,054	76	12.08	—

Runs	Wickets	Average	Best Analysis	5wI	10wM	Caught	Stumped
6	0	—	—	—	—	228	169

Number of Test Appearances: 1

As a young boy, Howard Levett liked the feel of a ball and would spend hours practising; taking the ball and catching – all this was at his prep school, before he even played in a match.

William Howard Vincent Levett, or 'Hopper' as he was known, was probably the second best wicket-keeper in the country in the mid-thirties – second only to Les Ames.

Levett made his county debut in 1930, his first game being against Worcestershire at Tunbridge Wells. He had the misfortune to drop Fox, the Worcestershire opener off 'Tich' Freeman, who was none too pleased! His first-class opportunity was somewhat restricted, but Kent were probably relieved that he was there. After a few years he began to keep wicket on a much more regular basis, especially after 1935, when a back injury to Ames limited his appearances behind the wicket.

In his debut season, 'Hopper' had dismissed 8 Lancashire batsmen in the fixture at Dover, 5 of them being stumped. In 1933 he went one better, helping to dismiss 9 Nottinghamshire batsmen in the match at Maidstone.

His chance of keeping wicket for England came at the end of that season, when he toured India with the MCC in 1933-34. He only played in one Test on that trip. It was at Calcutta, Levett scoring 5 and 2 and taking three catches.

'Hopper' was among the most colourful and lovable of Kent players; that he played only once for his country is a guide to the standard of wicket-keeping of his time. He was a source of encouragement to the bowlers, always urging them hard. He had days of brilliance when he was the best wicket-keeper in the land – the most inspiring of wicket-keepers.

In 1934 Levett dismissed 6 Nottinghamshire batsmen in one innings (4 caught, 2 stumped) and 9 in the match. He repeated this tally the following season in the match against Sussex at Tunbridge Wells. He equalled his highest number of dismissals in an innings, 6, when Kent played Glamorgan at Neath in 1939. All told, Levett dismissed 397 batsmen in his career with Kent. He dismissed 70 further batsmen in other first-class games.

Life was never dull when 'Hopper' was playing. At Canterbury in 1938, the Australians in their second innings only needed 7 to win. They sent in tail-enders and 'Hopper' was allowed to be the first Kent bowler. When he delivered the first 'ball', a bread roll arrived instead of the ball!

'Hopper' didn't mind the standard of cricket that he played. He appeared four times for the Gentlemen against the Players, but even if he was playing for the Second XI or representing a local club side on the village green, he always gave of his best. Renowned for his ability as a great talker, he did sterling work for the game, bridging the gap between the highest and lowest levels of the game.

As a batsman, he could certainly play straight, up and down the line. Occasionally he opened the innings for Kent, but he would often make valuable runs when needed.

The nickname of 'Hopper' originated from his captain, Percy Chapman. There was no connection with the Hopper's Tie Club which was founded much later than the time of Levett's career. His nickname of 'Hopper' was most appropriate because Howard Levett grew hops for a living and because his untidy appearance made Chapman think of a hop-picker!

'Hopper' was certainly one of the great characters of this wonderful game of cricket.

After a night on the tiles, it is reported that he remained totally motionless as the first ball of the morning and the match whistled past him for four byes. The batsman deflected the next delivery down the leg-side. Levett dived, caught it and came up triumphantly with the ball clutched firmly in his hand, saying 'Not bad for the first ball of the day, eh!'

Brian Luckhurst

Birthplace:	Sittingbourne, Kent
Born:	5 February 1939
Died:	
Played:	1958-1976

Averages in all first-class Kent matches:

Matches	Innings	Not Outs	Runs	Highest Score	Average	100s
335	568	65	19,096	215	38.00	39

Runs	Wickets	Average	Best Analysis	5wI	10wM	Catches
2,617	61	42.90	4 for 32	—	—	350

Number of Test Appearances: 21

Brian Luckhurst's cricket started one summer afternoon at Sittingbourne West Secondary Modern School, during a games lesson. His form master, Denis Jarrett, soon recognised the talent in the young cricketer who threw down his left arm deliveries. Within two years, Jarrett had the young Luckhurst flighting orthodox left-arm breaks and it was this that enabled him to break into the Gore Court First XI.

Kent were always on the look out for outstanding young cricketers and circulated schools. Denis Jarrett asked for Luckhurst to have a trial. He must have had a special talent because Claude Lewis, the then Kent coach, would give him a lift week after week to the Eltham nets for coaching.

On turning 15, Luckhurst left school to sit the Naval Dockyard entrance examinations. He was highly successful, but as Kent had offered him a position on the groundstaff there was only one choice for him.

Three years later he entered the Royal Artillery for his National Service. He played for the Army and Combined Services as an all-rounder, but by the time he returned to Kent, he was batting in the middle order and only bowling occasionally. He made his debut in the Kent First XI in 1958 at Worcester. On a rain-affected wicket he scored 23, but it was to be a good few years before he became a regular first teamer.

In 1962 he came into the side as a middle-order batsman, yet was still bowling his slow left-armers. That season he scored 1,096 runs at an average of 35.35 and took 4 for 32 at Gravesend in the match against Somerset. Wisden commented: 'Luckhurst, a dedicated youngster, looked a splendid prospect in his first full season. He showed praiseworthy determination, a sound defence and was also a fine fielder.'

In 1963 he scored 1,501 runs in the County Championship at an average of 33.35. By the following season he was batting at number three and occasionally opening, scoring 1,128 runs (average 31.33). In 1965 he slipped easily into the role of opening batsman, usually partnered by Mike Denness. Up to this season he was still playing football in the Medway League, but a broken collar bone made him realise that had the injury been more serious it could have ended his cricket career, so the football had to go!

As a batsman, Luckhurst was by nature an on-side player. He was very quick to move to the front foot and drove well on both sides of the wicket. In 1966 he scored 1,763 runs at an average of 35.26. The following season he hit hundreds against Hampshire, Northamptonshire and Sussex, but it was his contributions in Kent's successful Gillette Cup campaign that proved decisive. Perhaps his best batting exhibition came in the semi-final against Sussex at Canterbury, when he hit a superb 78. Also that season, with Sussex once again the opponents, he carried his bat for 126 out of Kent's total of 253 at Tunbridge Wells.

In 1968 Luckhurst scored 1,471 runs in Championship matches, hitting hundreds against Glamorgan, Hampshire and Somerset, but it was in Kent's match with the Rest of the World, when he scored 113 and 100 not out, that people began to sit up and take notice of this staunch county batsman. In 1969 Luckhurst scored 1,914 runs, his highest contribution in fourteen consecutive seasons of passing a thousand runs.

In Kent's Championship win of 1970, the turning point was yet another outstanding innings by Luckhurst. In two matches at Folkestone, Kent

collected 39 points. Yet when they faced Nottinghamshire on the second day of that week, Kent were struggling at 27 for 5 in reply to the Midland side's 376 for 4 declared. Enter Brian Luckhurst to hit a magnificent 156 not out and lead Kent to a remarkable victory. He hit the first of his double hundreds this season, 203 not out against Cambridge University at Fenners.

As a fielder Luckhurst was outstanding, especially in the backward square-leg position. He had an extraordinary strong left hand, often taking firm hits off fast bowlers, tossing the ball back quickly before the batsman realised he was out. In the match against Sussex that season he took six catches in the Hove fixture. This was also the season when Luckhurst was selected to represent England against the Rest of the World. In the second Test at Trent Bridge he hit an unbeaten 113, helping England to victory even though it did take him seven hours!

His official Test career began the following winter, when he played a vital part in Illingworth's Ashes-winning side. he batted with a new-found freedom, scoring 455 runs at an average of 56.87 in the five Tests, hitting hundreds at Melbourne and Perth.

The following summer Luckhurst led the way at the top of the Kent batting averages, scoring 1,368 runs at an average of 50.66. In 1972 he ended the season with his highest average in the County Championship, 64.85.

In 1973 he helped Graham Johnson put on 256 for the first wicket at Derby. It was in this match that he hit the highest score of his career; 215. Kent marked Les Ames's retirement as manager by winning the Gillette Cup for the second time. In the quarter-final against Leicestershire, Luckhurst hit 125 as Kent scored 295 for 8, only two runs short of their highest score in the competition. Leicestershire were the county to suffer again at the hands of 'Lucky' as he hit a superb 111 in the Benson and Hedges quarter-final, though this time the side from Grace Road won by 8 runs.

In England's next confrontation with Australia, Luckhurst's Test career was dimmed by the pace of Lillee. Yet it had been Luckhurst who made England's highest score (96) against Lillee and Massie. He played in 21 Tests for England, scoring 1,298 runs at an average of 36.05.

In 1975 Luckhurst passed the thousand-run mark for the last time, scoring 1,180 runs at an average of 31.89.

In 1976 Luckhurst's magnificent contribution to Kent first-team cricket ended when he broke his finger at Maidstone in the match against Northamptonshire. He then became captain of the Second XI, helping the younger players in their preparation for the step to first-class cricket. In the winter months he had worked for both the Atlantic Petroleum Oil Company and on the administrative staff of Lillywhite Frowd.

At one time Luckhurst was Kent manager, but the man who achieved all the honours in the game now holds the post of Kent Cricket Administrator.

Charles Marriott

Birthplace:	Heaton Moor, Lancashire
Born:	14 September 1895
Died:	13 October 1966
Played:	1924-1937

Averages in all first-class Kent matches:

Matches	Innings	Not Outs	Runs	Highest Score	Average	100s
101	105	31	356	21	4.81	—

Runs	Wickets	Average	Best Analysis	5wI	10wM	Catches
9,391	463	20.28	7 for 52	32	8	26

Number of Test Appearances: 1

Charles Stowell Marriott was born in Lancashire, but brought up in Ireland and educated at St Columba's. It was here that he learned his cricket.

From 1919 to 1921 he appeared for Lancashire. When he made his Lancashire debut in May 1919 against Essex at Leyton, it was the first time that he had ever been present at a county game!

He studied at Cambridge University, where he gained a Blue in 1920 and 1921. He met with remarkable success in the University games. In 1920, when rain had prevented play on the first two days, he took 7 for 69. In the following season he played a leading role as Cambridge beat rivals Oxford, taking 7 for 111 in the match, bowling fastish leg-breaks on the perfect Fenner's pitch.

In 1921 he was chosen in the squad for the Old Trafford Test, but was eventually left out.

After his three seasons with Lancashire, he took a job at Dulwich College as master-in-charge of cricket. Thereafter he played for Kent during the summer holidays. He went on to make his Kent debut in 1924 and begin his link with 'Tich' Freeman that was to become the deadliest leg-break combination that English county cricket was ever to know. For Marriott, his partnership with 'Tich' was the delight of his cricketing life.

In that first season with Kent he distinguished himself by taking 5 for 31 and 6 for 48 in the game at Dover against Lancashire. Later that year at Canterbury, he took 5 for 66 and 5 for 44 in the match against Hampshire.

'Father' Marriott, as he was popularly known, went on two tours abroad. The first in 1924-25 when he went on Lord Tennyson's trip to South Africa.

In 1933 Marriott took 54 wickets at 18.44 runs each. This was the season when he played in his one and only Test match, against the West Indies at the Oval. That he was picked at all was a magnificent tribute to his skill as a bowler, because he was an unbelievably bad batsman and was wholly unathletic in the field.

His debut was a sensational one; his first over being a maiden to the great George Headley. He then proceeded to bewilder the West Indians as he took 5 for 37 in their first innings. In the second innings he had figures of 6 for 59, as West Indies were defeated by an innings and 17 runs. It was a feat described by Wisden of the time as one of the best accomplished by a bowler when playing for England for the first time. That he only played in one Test match for his country, despite his skill as a spinner, notably from leg, was very surprising!

In 1933-34 he went with D R Jardine's MCC team to India. he didn't play in a Test match, but in the fixture against Madras he did the hat-trick for the only time in his first-class career.

C S Marriott had long loose arms and long sensitive fingers. His action was high, with the free loose arm swung behind his back, hitting it so hard that the batsman heard the slap! He bowled at nearly medium-pace and with great accuracy. He relied heavily on the leg-break, the top-spinner

128

and, surprisingly, the off-break which he regarded as a better bet than the googly. He would only use the googly once or twice at the start of his bowling spell – this was to please 'Tich' Freeman, who often bowled a googly first delivery to a new batsman. In fact, of the two bowlers, many good batsmen of the time preferred to face Freeman!

He played his last game for Kent in 1937, when he went back to his post as a school-master. During the Second World War he served as an anti-aircraft gunner in the Home Guard.

In all first-class matches he took 724 wickets at an average cost of 20.04 runs each. His skill as a bowler far outshone his ability as a batsman, as he only scored 555 runs in his career. He had just completed a book called *The Complete Leg-Break Bowler* when he died in October 1966, a man of great charm, loved by everyone.

Jack Mason

Birthplace:	Blackheath, London
Born:	29 October 1873
Died:	15 October 1958
Played:	1893-1914

Averages in all first-class Kent matches:

Matches	Innings	Not Outs	Runs	Highest Score	Average	100s
300	491	33	15,563	183	33.98	31

Runs	Wickets	Average	Best Analysis	5wI	10wM	Catches
16,969	769	22.06	8 for 29	31	9	360

Number of Test Appearances: 5

John Richard Mason was educated at Winchester. Even in his schooldays he began to show his ability as an all-rounder. In 1892, in the match against Eton, he scored 147 and 71, dismissed 8 batsmen and took three catches. The following season in the corresponding fixture, he scored 43 and 36, and again took 8 wickets. His record for Winchester in 1892 was 777 runs at an average of 48.00 and 48 wickets at 18 runs apiece. The following year, his record was 719 runs (average 55.00) and 45 wickets for under 17 runs apiece.

In the same season he stepped straight out of the Winchester XI and into the Kent side. He played in the game against the touring Australians, when Kent beat the tourists by 36 runs. He disappointed the following season, but in 1895 he hit 1,137 runs at an average of 30.73. For the next few years he continued to give good all-round service and in 1897 he went with A E Stoddart's side to Australia. He took part in all five Test matches, but nothing shows more clearly the strength of English cricket at that time, because Mason never played in a Test in England. The nearest he came to it was in 1902, when he was one of the fourteen players from whom the final eleven would be selected at the Edgbaston Test. Jack Mason is often quoted as the best player never to represent England in this country. He appeared for the Gentlemen against the Players in 1894 and 1895 and from 1897 to 1902. In the match at Lord's Mason was batting with W G Grace. They had put on 130 runs, with WG on 78, when Mason called him for a short run. WG was run out, Mason forgetting the great man's age and weight!

In 1898 he succeeded Frank Marchant as Kent captain. He led the county well for the next five years and would have done so for much longer had not the calls of his profession as a solicitor necessitated his resignation. Mason played on a regular basis until 1906; from then, until war broke out, he played only infrequently.

In 1899 he shared in what is still a third wicket record stand for Kent. Batting with Alec Hearne against Nottinghamshire at Trent Bridge, he helped to put on 321 runs. Although comparatively brief, his career was outstanding.

In 1900 he scored 1,662 runs at an average of 53.61 and took 78 wickets at around 19 runs apiece. His best match was against Middlesex at Tonbridge, when he scored 72 and 46 not out and took 10 for 57. Against Surrey at the Oval he scored 98 and 147.

In 1901 he scored 1,467 runs (average 39.64) and took 92 wickets at around 20 runs apiece. In the match against Somerset at Taunton, Mason scored 145 and took 12 for 55, bowling unchanged with Colin Blythe.

In 1904 Mason hit three centuries in successive matches. Against Yorkshire he notched up 138 and followed it with 126 in the match at Beckenham against Somerset (he also took 10 for 180 in the match). His third century, 133, came against Essex. Also in the reverse fixture against Somerset at Taunton, Mason scored 100 and took 10 for 81. The following year Somerset were again the county to suffer, as Mason hit 133 and took 10 for 222 in the match at Taunton. In the same season at the Oval, he took 7 catches to add to his all-rounder tag!

In 1909 Mason topped the first-class batting averages in what was a summer of wet wickets.

Jack Mason was primarily a forward player, possessing a powerful drive and a most effective cut. At well over six feet in height, he made full use of

130

it, always playing with a straight bat. As a bowler, he had a model action and a high arm, making the ball run away. He bowled at a fast-medium pace, verging more on fast. There have also been few greater slip fielders. Mason would be part of a slip cordon which included Hutchings and Seymour. It has been said that after a catch had been taken, the ball would be passed from one to another so quickly that often the scorer couldn't tell who had caught it.

Altogether he hit 15,563 runs, took 769 wickets and held 360 catches – one of the finest amateur all-rounders to play for Kent.

In 1938 he became President of the Kent County Cricket Club. He died in October 1958 at the age of 84, one of the most popular and respected of Kent players.

Arthur Phebey

Birthplace:	Catford, London	
Born:	1 October 1924	
Died:		
Played:	1946-1961	

Averages in all first-class Kent matches:

Matches	Innings	Not Outs	Runs	Highest Score	Average	100s
320	585	33	14,299	157	25.90	12

Runs	Wickets	Average	Best Analysis	5wI	10wM	Catches
4	0	—	—	—	—	202

Number of Test Appearances: 0

Arthur Phebey made a very promising start for Kent County Cricket Club when the game resumed after the Second World War. He then decided to leave the staff for a time, losing much valuable experience.

After returning to the fold, it was 1951 before he established himself fully in the side. He carried his bat on four occasions, his best effort being 89 out of Kent's 209 against Worcestershire at Kidderminster that year.

Phebey was an elegant opening batsman. He helped bring solidarity to the Kent batting line-up. He was a very good example of what a straight bat and correct style can achieve. There were other batsmen in the Kent side and indeed in county cricket in general who had far greater natural ability than Phebey, but few made as many runs.

Opening the Kent batting, he achieved over 1,000 runs a season for nine consecutive years. The first of these was 1952, when he scored 1,042 runs at an average of 25.41. The next two seasons saw him score over 1,300 runs in the County Championship; 1,314 in 1953 (average 25.26) and 1,313 in 1954 (average 26.26). In 1955 he scored 1,014 runs at an average of 23.58, including 122 at Northampton. He continued to score over a thousand runs a season for Kent, yet was never considered to represent his country, though he was a most reliable county opening batsman.

In 1957 he scored 1,576 runs (average 29.18), including a well hit 111 at Folkestone against Worcestershire. His best season in terms of runs scored in the County Championship was 1959, when he totalled 1,737 runs at an average of 33.40.

The following season he shared in the second highest partnership for Kent's third wicket with his opening partner, the adventurous left-hander Robert Wilson. They put 304 runs on for the third wicket in the match

against Glamorgan at Blackheath. They were a very good opening partnership for Kent for many years.

Phebey retired at the end of the 1961 season, when he must have had a good few years of first-class cricket still in him. In first-class matches for Kent, he scored 14,299 runs at an average of 25.90 and with a top score of 157.

He is still heavily involved with Kent cricket, being a member of the General Committee, elected for four years in 1989, and the Executive Committee. A belated honour came his way when he was one of four Life Vice-Presidents appointed last year.

Fred Ridgway

Birthplace:	Stockport, Cheshire	
Born:	10 August 1923	
Died:		
Played:	1946-1961	

Averages in all first-class Kent matches:

Matches	Innings	Not Outs	Runs	Highest Score	Average	100s
298	442	100	3,812	94	11.14	—

Runs	Wickets	Average	Best Analysis	5wI	10wM	Catches
22,740	955	23.81	8 for 39	38	6	203

Number of Test Appearances: 5

Frederick Ridgway made his debut for the Kent First XI in 1946, although it was some three years later that he showed his worth.

He was a great trier and, though never truly fast, he could certainly be hostile. He often had to bowl long spells without a rest and this he did cheerfully. Taking this into consideration it isn't surprising that often his bowling figures were quite expensive.

In 1949 he had his most successful season in terms of taking wickets. In all first-class matches, he took 105 wickets at a cost of 23.32 runs each. This season he also showed his worth with the bat. He shared in what is presently the Kent ninth wicket partnership record, putting on 161 with B R Edrich in the match against Sussex at Tunbridge Wells, Ridgway ending with 89 runs to his name.

In 1951, in the match against Derbyshire, Ridgway became the first Kent bowler since 1862 to take 4 wickets in four balls. His final figures in this match at Folkestone were 6 for 44. The events leading up to this fine performance are worth recording. The wicket was a good one for batsmen, and Donald Carr and Revill had put 159 runs on when the new ball became available. Uncharacteristically, Ridgway showed no enthusiasm for taking it. He was forced to do so and what happened next is quite remarkable. With the first ball of his second over, he bowled Revill with a half-volley. The second ball accounted for Kelly, Arthur Fagg taking a catch in the slips. The third and hat-trick ball had Rhodes caught by Cowdrey at fine-leg and the fourth had Gladwin taken by Evans behind the wickets.

Ridgway was in his prime when many other quick bowlers were available for England to choose. However, he was chosen for the MCC tour of India in 1951-52. He seemed an ideal choice, being able to bowl for a long time. He was also short in stature and so some of his deliveries kept rather low. He played in five Tests on that tour, but only took 7 wickets at the high cost of 54.14 runs each, and although he was a useful lower-order batsman, he only managed 49 runs in the Tests at an average of 8.16.

There is another example of Ridgway disappointing with his opening spell, but coming out on top when he came back for a second bite. In the 1952 encounter between Kent and Essex at Clacton, Dickie Dodds, the Essex opener, had taken Ridgway apart; his figures at the end of his first spell were 0 for 60. His second spell was a completely different story. His fine accurate bowling resulted in his final analysis being 8 for 112.

Also that season in Kent's fixture against the Indian tourists, there was an occurrence which one hopes was a one-off. The Indian Test player, Umrigar, had hammered the Kent bowling to all parts of the St Lawrence Ground and went on to make 204. Ridgway lost his control and, after running in to bowl, he threw the ball deliberately at Umrigar. He wasn't no-balled because umpire Skelding at square-leg wasn't paying attention!

In his later years, when he'd lost some of his pace, he increased his control and therefore became a much better bowler. In 1958 he took 7 for 42 against Oxford University, including the second hat-trick of his career. His best figures were 8 for 39 against Gloucestershire.

He played his last game for the county in 1961. A great trier, Fred Ridgway possesses an unwanted distinction. As he ran in to deliver his first ball before the Queen, he fell flat on his face!

James Seymour

Birthplace: West Hoathly, Sussex
Born: 25 October 1879
Died: 30 September 1930
Played: 1902-1926

Averages in all first-class Kent matches:

Matches	Innings	Not Outs	Runs	Highest Score	Average	100s
536	881	60	26,818	218*	32.62	53

Runs	Wickets	Average	Best Analysis	5wI	10wM	Catches
680	15	45.33	4 for 62	—	—	659

Number of Test Appearances: 0

Jim Seymour was born in Sussex but, due to his long residence in Pembury, he became eligible to play for Kent. In 1900 he was engaged to play for the London County Cricket Club. Also during that summer he played an innings of 66 not out for Kent Club and Ground against Gravesend and was offered a place on the ground staff at Tonbridge. It was here that he developed his skill as a batsman, through the coaching of Captain W McCanlis.

His first season as a regular in the Kent First XI was 1902, though it was some two years later before he made his mark. In 1904 he scored 1,166 runs at an average of 28.43, including two hundreds, 108 and 136 not out at Maidstone in the match against Worcestershire.

As a slip fielder, he was on a par with the greatest to occupy this position, the combination of Huish, Seymour, Mason, Blaker and Hutchings behind the wickets being one of the most difficult to pass. In 1904, whilst fielding in the slips, Seymour caught six of the touring South African team in the match at Canterbury and six against Yorkshire at Hull the following season.

In 1905 he scored 1,471 runs (average 34.20). It was during this summer that he shared in a second wicket partnership of 261 with Edward Dillon in the match against Somerset at Taunton. When, in 1906, Kent won the County Championship, Jim Seymour scored 1,096 runs and was the leading professional batsman of the XI. He played a superb innings of 204 against Hampshire at Tonbridge in 1907, setting a new record for Kent at the time. In total that season he scored 1,547 runs at an average of 35.97. He continued to top the thousand-run mark for the next three seasons, and in 1911 he repeated his double century of four years earlier. He exceeded his past score when he hit an unbeaten 218 against Essex at Leyton. The following year, along with 1925, were the only two seasons that Seymour failed to reach the 1,000 runs in a season between 1904 and 1926.

In 1913 he had a great season, finishing with an aggregate of 2,088 runs and an average of just under 40. He never took part in a Test and appeared in only three Gentlemen v Players matches. It was in this season that he played in the first of these three matches, making 80 in the second innings at the Oval. The following season, the last before the war, saw Seymour scoring 1,404 runs, including 214 against Essex at Tunbridge Wells.

Seymour never rose to the highest level of representative cricket because in his day the standard was very high indeed, yet he was a player of the highest class in terms of county cricket. In those days it was probably very difficult to select the best XI for Kent, but one thing was certain, Jim Seymour could never be left out!

He was a superb player. He played with an upright, yet slightly open stance, possessing probably the widest range of strokes of any batsman in England. His flash past cover-point was a pure delight and he excelled also at the old-fashioned full-blooded leg-side hit. Occasionally he didn't always appear sure of himself in facing fast bowling, yet there were few players more watchful than Seymour when facing the ball on a turning wicket.

In 1922 he had his most successful season, especially in terms of his batting average, 47.97. He shared in two productive partnerships, 307 with Wally Hardinge against Worcestershire and 280 with Frank Woolley

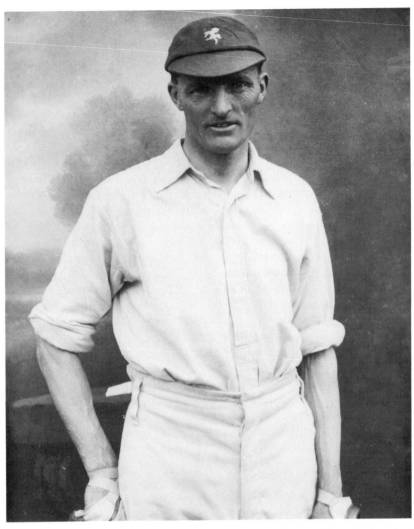

against Lancashire at Dover. Yet, three consecutive matches during that summer show Jim Seymour's attitude to the game.

At Southend, against Essex, Kent were attempting to save the game, but lost Hardinge at 12. Seymour walked to the wicket and proceeded to hit the first ball he faced from Douglas over square-leg for 4. He scored 90 to save the game for Kent, justifying his shot off that first ball by saying: 'I thought Colonel Douglas looked dangerous.' At the Oval against Surrey, Kent needed 247 runs to save an innings defeat. Seymour made 98 glorious runs in the first eighty minutes, Kent finishing 228 runs ahead and with 3 wickets in hand. Seymour scored 80 out of 117 runs, never being in trouble.

138

The following season, 1923, he scored hundreds in each innings, Essex yet again the side to suffer as Seymour scored 143 and 105 not out in the fixture at Leyton.

After retiring from the first class scene in 1926, he became a hero to every professional cricketer.

Seymour received a demand for income tax on that part of his benefit money which accrued from entry fees paid at the gate. Fortunately, on appeal, the Income Tax Commissioners decided in his favour. The Crown took the case to the High Court, where the Commissioners' decision was upheld. The Crown then appealed to the Court of Appeal and won. Seymour appealed to the Lords and won his case!

He then accepted an engagement as coach at Epsom College, but died some four years later at Marden, aged 50.

John Shepherd

Birthplace:	Belleplaine, Barbados
Born:	9 November 1943
Died:	
Played:	1966-1981

Averages in all first-class Kent matches:

Matches	Innings	Not Outs	Runs	Highest Score	Average	100s
303	431	74	9,401	170	26.33	8

Runs	Wickets	Average	Best Analysis	5wI	10wM	Catches
22,106	832	26.56	8 for 83	45	2	212

Number of Test Appearances: 5

John Shepherd originates from the parish of St Andrew on the eastern side of the island of Barbados. He attended Alleyn's School, where his schoolboy hero was Everton Weekes.

In 1964 Colin Cowdrey and Les Ames were touring the West Indies when they came across a good young cricketer with a super personality; his name of course, John Shepherd. They invited him to come to England and play for the Second XI at Kent. As a young player it was a big step for him but he soon settled in, adapting to his new life in England. Within two years he had established himself in the Kent First XI.

139

He made his debut in the Kent side in 1966 and was awarded his county cap the following year. It was in 1967 that Kent won the Gillette Cup, Shepherd making an important contribution in the semi-final match against Sussex at Canterbury. Batting at number three he made a quick-fire 77.

In the close season he returned to the West Indies to play for Barbados in the Shell Shield. Perhaps he was hoping to force his way into the West Indies side to oppose the MCC team, captained by Colin Cowdrey – I would certainly have thought so. It wasn't to be. In the first match of the tour he hooked a short-pitched delivery from Warwickshire's David Brown, it flew off the edge of his bat and into his face, breaking his cheekbone. Shepherd missed most of that season; he did come back towards the end of it, but much too late to be considered for the West Indies' Test team.

In 1968 Kent were runners-up in the County Championship, Shepherd making a great impression in his first full season. He scored 1,157 runs at an average of 29.66 and took 96 wickets, bowling at a very economical medium-pace style. With the bat he hit 170 against Northamptonshire at Folkestone, following it with hundreds against Middlesex and Hampshire. With the ball he was always a threat, taking 6 for 60 against Warwickshire at Canterbury. He took 5 wickets on five occasions in the County Championship, Lancashire, Glamorgan (twice), Somerset and Northamptonshire being the teams to suffer.

In 1969 the West Indies were the side touring England and John Shepherd was an automatic choice. He ended the Test series by playing in each Test, topping the Test bowling averages. In the first Test at Old Trafford, Shepherd bowled 58 overs in England's first innings, taking 5 for 104. At the end of the three-match series he had taken 12 wickets at a cost of 22.16 runs each.

In 1970 Kent celebrated their centenary year by winning the County Championship. Shepherd took more wickets than any other Kent bowler: 84. He backed this up by scoring 700 runs and fielding brilliantly throughout the season. One match that season against Leicestershire at Folkestone, Shepherd was to more than prove his worth. He bowled a devastating second spell at a time when Leicestershire, after winning the toss, were threatening to take control. At 102 for 3, Shepherd was brought back into the attack and Leicestershire slumped to 127 for 8, eventually being bowled out for 152. Leicestershire's dangermen, Clive Inman and Peter Marner, were dismissed in a spell of 4 for 9 in just twenty-one deliveries by Shepherd. It was a beautiful piece of bowling on a good wicket.

Shepherd returned home to play in two further Tests against India. He took 7 wickets, but they were to be his last. Surprisingly, the West Indies

didn't seem able to come to terms with his obvious talents. He wasn't selected to tour Australia or the next tour of England.

In a Gillette Cup quarter-final match of 1972 against Essex at Leyton, Shepherd quite unbelievably missed out on the Man-of-the-Match medal. Kent had been dismissed for only 137, with Asif scoring 52. Essex had reached 55 without loss, when Shepherd took 4 wickets without conceding a run, Kent eventually winning by 10 runs, Essex being all out for 127.

In 1973 Shepherd had a splendid all-round season and wasn't far short of the 'double', despite the reduction of the first-class programme.

He also became the first black cricketer to tour South Africa with the Derrick Robins team. In 1975-76 he played for Rhodesia in the Currie Cup. He also had successful seasons playing Grade Cricket for Footscray, the Melbourne club, picking up more runs and wickets than anyone else.

In the 1975 County Championship, Shepherd bowled more overs than anyone, his best figures being 15 for 147 against Sussex at Maidstone.

In 1977 Kent shared the County Championship with Middlesex. John Shepherd was the main contributor to the Kent efforts in bowling a side out twice. His seamers took 87 wickets at a cost of under 20 runs apiece. That was forty more than any of his colleagues. On six occasions he took 5 or more wickets in an innings, including a best for Kent of 8 for 83 against Lancashire at Tunbridge Wells.

In 1979 this well loved and respected cricketer was awarded a well-deserved benefit.

He is probably the best of his type of bowler that Kent have had on their staff since the war. Quickish, he could swing the ball both ways, move it off the seam and he possessed an extremely good fast delivery.

After the end of the 1981 season he moved on the Gloucestershire where, after a few seasons, he became their coach. John Shepherd was a great player for Kent, a man who always cared deeply about pride of performance and one that always had time for people.

Chris Tavare

Birthplace:	Orpington, Kent
Born:	27 October 1954
Died:	
Played:	1974-1988

Averages in all first-class Kent matches:

Matches	Innings	Not Outs	Runs	Highest Score	Average	100s
259	425	51	14,201	168*	37.97	29

Runs	Wickets	Average	Best Analysis	5wI	10wM	Catches
493	5	98.60	1 for 20	—	—	269

Number of Test Appearances: 30

Chris Tavare was educated at Sevenoaks School and Oxford University, where he gained a Zoology degree. It was obvious at Oxford that Tavare was destined for a great career in both county and international cricket. He won the respect of the opposing professionals with his disciplined approach to his batting. He won Blues at Oxford from 1975 to 1977, although in 1973 he hit a hundred for the English Schools against All India Schools at Edgbaston, and made his Kent debut in 1974. After hitting centuries for Oxford, he hit his first hundred: 124 for Kent, in 1977 in the match against Nottinghamshire at Canterbury.

In his first full season for Kent in 1978, he scored 1,432 runs in the County Championship at an average of 44.75. Tavare was the ideal number three for Kent. He was a remarkably consistent batsman, who could both anchor an innings or give Kent a push with his stylish stroke play. It was evident in these early years that Kent were soon going to be losing him to England for Test matches.

Also in 1978 Tavare held 48 catches in only 24 matches, a Kent record. His average of two catches per match represents quite an achievement.

In 1979 he scored 1,239 runs at an average of 39.96. He helped Alan Ealham put on 251 for the fourth wicket in the match against Worcestershire at Canterbury. In the Tunbridge Wells week, he showed his ability to concentrate for long periods by hitting 150 not out against Essex. The following season Tavare got his first chance at a higher level when he was chosen to represent England in the one-day international against the West Indies. The match was at Headingley, Tavare scoring 82 not out. This fine innings won him selection for the first two Tests. In his second Test, he scored 42 at Lord's, but it was considered too slow and without strokes worthy of this high level! Yet twelve months later, the same people were grateful for his contribution.

In 1981 Tavare scored 1,591 runs (average 54.86), his best season to date. When he was recalled to the England ranks for the Test at Old Trafford he played two important innings of 69 and 78. In the match he batted for something like twelve hours, his second 50 being the slowest in a Test in England at the time. Yet England were grateful for his contributions on this occasion.

Also in 1981 Tavare showed the other side of his batting technique. In the Lambert and Butler Floodlit Cup at Crystal Palace's Football Ground, he hit a century off just 27 balls!

In 1981-82 Tavare toured India where he scored his first Test hundred: 149 at Delhi. He finished that series with 349 runs at an average of 38.77. In the first meeting of England and Sri Lanka at Colombo, he hit a vital 85 in England's second innings.

In 1982 he helped Alan Knott put on an unbeaten 256 in a defiant stand for the sixth wicket in the match against Essex at Chelmsford. Though he batted at number three for Kent, the England selectors asked him to open. This he did and at Lord's in the Test against Pakistan he 'broke' (if that's the right word!) his record, when he took some 350 minutes to reach his 50. His innings of 82 in just over 400 minutes almost saved England from defeat and showed his skill, courage and concentration at the highest level.

The tour of Australia in 1982-83 wasn't a successful one for Tavare, but on his return to England he was appointed Kent's captain. He was also captain in 1984, when he hit 1,119 runs at an average of 29.44. During his captaincy he led Kent to two losing Lord's finals. When he lost the captaincy he was greatly upset and it was thought he might leave the county. Instead, he signed a new four-year contract and buckled down to score over 1,000 runs in each of those four years. In 1985 he scored 1,225 runs (average 36.02) and 1,267 runs (average 33.34) in 1986. The following season he hit 1,167 runs at an average of 33.05. He helped Mark Benson put on 285 for the third wicket against Worcestershire at New Road.

In his last season with Kent he scored 1,430 runs at an average of 42.05 and his experience and application helped the county to within one point of the County Championship.

At the start of 1989 Tavare left the county to join Somerset on a one-year contract. Married to a Somerset girl and always batting well at Taunton, he settled in well, scoring 1,292 runs in the Championship. His one-day form was outstanding, averaging 115.33 in the Benson and Hedges Cup and 180.00 in the Nat West Trophy.

His departure to the West County left a void in the Kent line-up, but his fifteen years of skill and sportsmanship were enjoyed by many.

Charles Thornton

Birthplace:	Llanwarne, Hereford
Born:	20 March 1850
Died:	10 December 1929
Played:	1867-1872

Averages in all first-class Kent matches:

Matches	Innings	Not Outs	Runs	Highest Score	Average	100s
18	34	1	959	124	29.06	3

Runs	Wickets	Average	Best Analysis	5wI	10wM	Caught
205	8	25.62	2 for 12	—	—	12

Number of Test Appearances: 0

Charles Inglis Thornton was born at Llanwarne, Hereford, the son of a rector. He went to Eton in 1861, playing cricket for the XI in 1866, 1867 and 1868, in which he was captain. It was whilst he was at Eton that he began to show his sporting prowess. He won the school Fives, the Double Racquets, Putting the Weight and Throwing the Cricket Ball. After going up to Trinity College, Cambridge, he played in the XI for four years, 1869-1872, the last year as captain.

In the year he went up to Cambridge, Thornton was a fast under-arm bowler and once, when playing for his own XI against King's School, Canterbury, his 'sneaks' took all 10 wickets!

At the Oval his 'sneaks' had the Surrey crowd in uproar after he claimed three Surrey favourites' wickets. Willisher, the old Kent bowler calmed the spectators, but Thornton finished with 4 for 34 as Surrey were dismissed for 310. Between the years 1866 and 1871, he took somewhere in the region of 600 wickets, though only a few for Kent!

He was a real character and is probably the biggest hitter English cricket has ever had. He delighted in big hits, whether it be the first ball or last ball of a match. He once challenged Lord Harris to a duel to see who could hit the ball the furthest. Lord Harris hit one delivery into the pavilion. The following over saw Thornton hit the same bowler over the players' dressing-room to win the challenge!

In those days it was quite common to measure drives. It was not uncommon for Thornton to hit some 140 or 150 yards. In fact, one of his hits at Canterbury was such a colossal drive that it measured 152 yards. He also cleared the old Lord's pavilion when representing Eton in 1868 and followed this with a similar shot over the Oval pavilion which was also later replaced. Thornton's largest measured hit was just short of 169 yards, made at Hove. He was practising in front of the pavilion, when the ball was lobbed up to him and eventually finished in the road past the entrance gates. Cricket historian, The Reverend James Pycroft, was just about to enter the ground and marked the exact spot where the ball landed and measured the distance.

He once hit nine sixes over the canvas at Tunbridge Wells (it enclosed the ground), and at Canterbury he hit each ball of one over from V E Walker (they were four-ball overs) out of the ground!

Without doubt, Scarborough was Thornton's favourite ground. It was here that he played his best innings when representing the Gentlemen of England against I Zingari in 1886. When he went in to bat, the Gentlemen were 133 for 5; when the innings closed on 266, Thornton was left on 107 not out. In 1894 Thornton was presented with a silver loving-cup subscribed for by the members of Scarborough Cricket Club. In 1921 he was made a Freeman of the Borough of Scarborough, where he organised several games and was, in the main, responsible for the introduction of the cricket festival there.

On one occasion at Scarborough, off the bowling of Lancashire's A G Steel, he drove a ball over a four-storeyed house into the adjoining street, called Trafalgar Square. The stories all have slight variations! When Thornton was asked whether he hit it from Lord's or the Oval, he replied: 'It was from the Oval and it went via Westminster Bridge!'

Like many players of his day, Thornton regarded cricket purely as a game rather than the serious business it has become today. Whenever he captained a side, he liked going in first. He would jump quickly to the delivery, and make magnificent drives. In his brilliant career he put together many scores of 100 in remarkable time.

To show the difference between cricket in Thornton's day and now: he took part in six seasons for Kent, in only 18 matches. In his 34 innings he hit three hundreds. Thornton never wore pads and only wore gloves (and then only one) towards the end of his career.

Thornton was also an avid film goer and used to carry an enormous black wallet containing newspaper reports on every murder case for the past twenty-five years!

He had to be watched when the coin was tossed. Thornton used to call 'Woman', which could be either heads (Queen Victoria) or tails (Britannia), and before the other captain had realised what was happening, Thornton would have decided to bat!

In business, Thornton was in the timber trade for thirty-five years, retiring in 1912. He was also a keen motorist and after he'd finished playing cricket he travelled through Japan, Siberia and Russia. When the war broke out he was in Berlin and just avoided being captured.

He died suddenly in Marylebone, London, in 1929 at the age of 79. With his death there passed a great personality in the history of cricket.

Leslie Todd

Birthplace: Catford, London
Born: 19 June 1907
Died: 20 August 1967
Played: 1927-1950

Averages in all first-class Kent matches:

Matches	Innings	Not Outs	Runs	Highest Score	Average	100s
426	709	93	19,407	174	31.50	36

Runs	Wickets	Average	Best Analysis	5wI	10wM	Catches
15,197	555	27.38	6 for 26	20	1	226

Number of Test Appearances: 0

When Leslie Todd entered county cricket with Kent in 1927, he was hailed as another Frank Woolley. Yet he was probably the game's greatest enigma.

When runs were needed quickly to gain advantage, Todd would keep one end completely shut up. If it was vital that Kent didn't lose another wicket, he would set about the bowling, unleashing an array of unorthodox strokes and more than likely get out! His captain and teammates were obviously furious, but nobody was angry with him for long.

His stroke play was certainly varied; he had a strong defence, but was often prone to play flashing shots. He often failed to make the most of his talents because he had the most extraordinary of tempers. In the early thirties, he began to pass the one-thousand runs a season mark. From 1933 until the outbreak of the Second World War he succeeded in reaching this goal with the exception of 1938. His best season was 1934 when he scored 1,897 runs in the County Championship at an average of 52.69 runs.

In 1936 Todd did the cricketer's 'double'. He scored 1,211 runs (average 26.91) and took 102 wickets (average 21.05 runs each). During that season Toddie was often the despair of his captain, Percy Chapman. In the match against Glamorgan at Folkestone, Todd displayed the infuriating side of his nature. Kent were after some quick runs, but Todd had been in some two-and-a-half hours before completing his 50. Chapman sent in Levett with the message: 'Get a hundred or you are dropped for the next match.' Levett was soon dismissed and though Chapman, Lewis and Watt all made a few runs, it was left to 'Tich' Freeman to stay with Todd. When 'Tich' joined him he was on 69 but the little man kept his end tight, Todd eventually going for 113.

Percy Chapman was probably the ideal captain to handle Todd's antics. In one match, Kent were in difficulties when Chapman joined Todd in the middle. 'All right skipper; I'll look after one end, you play your natural game.' Not too many captains would have accepted this with such good humour.

Todd was also a fine fielder, especially if there was the chance to show off his talent for the spectacular stop!

Todd was a complete all-rounder. As a bowler, he was intially a slow bowler, though in the seasons prior to the war he bowled left-arm medium-quick, with a devilish late in-swinger. In the County Championship he took 555 wickets at a cost of 27.38 runs, his best figures being 6 for 26.

When cricket resumed after the war, Todd did little bowling because he had back trouble.

Despite his temperament and the loss of six years to the Second World War when he was at his peak, he still surpassed 20,000 runs in all forms of cricket.

In 1947 Todd amassed 2,057 runs in the County Championship at an average of 44.71 runs. He also shared in a second-wicket stand of 273 with Les Ames in the match against Essex at Maidstone. In all County Championship matches, Todd scored 19,407 runs at an average of 31.50 and with a top score of 174.

Few players have had such talent for the game of cricket, yet Leslie Todd never played for England. The closest he came to gaining representative honours was one appearance in a Test trial but, unfortunately, he didn't do himself justice.

Kent could, and did, accommodate this wayward genious, but the Test selectors were a little wary of choosing someone whose approach to cricket was, to say the least, unpredictable.

Leslie Todd was perhaps the most infuriating and peverse cricketer of his time.

Lionel Troughton

Birthplace:	Seaford, Sussex
Born:	17 May 1879
Died:	3 August 1933
Played:	1907-1923

Averages in all first-class Kent matches:

Matches	Innings	Not Outs	Runs	Highest Score	Average	100s
164	235	30	3,477	104	16.96	1

Runs	Wickets	Average	Best Analysis	5wI	10wM	Catches
20	0	—	—	—	—	72

Number of Test Appearances: 0

Lionel Holmes Wood Troughton was a member of the Dulwich College First XI in 1897 and made his debut for the Kent Second XI some three years later in 1900. He first played for the Kent First XI in 1907, but over the next few seasons he fluctuated between the First and Second XIs. Towards the beginning of the First World War, sides were becoming more professional.

One result of this shortage of amateur players was when E W Dillon resigned the captaincy after the successful season of 1913, and Kent appointed Lionel Troughton. Troughton hadn't even had an assured spot in the Kent First XI and hadn't even been awared his county cap. In fact, at the time of his appointment Troughton was captain of the Kent Second XI. However, his appointment was a popular decision; Troughton was a most respected captain.

During that season of his captaincy, he scored 776 runs. He also hit the only century of his career in the fixture against Oxford University. In reply to Oxford's 337, Kent scored 571, Troughton's share being 104.

During the war he had a fine record, holding the position of Lieutenant-Colonel.

In 1921 Troughton had his second most successful season, when he scored 761 runs. He held the position of captain until 1923, when he handed the job over to Captain (later Lord) Cornwallis. Troughton himself took over the post of business manager at Kent that same year, when the beloved Tom Pawley died at Canterbury at the beginning of August.

Lionel Troughton was never a very prolific scoring batsman, though he often made useful scores when he batted around number seven or eight. He was a very capable captain, which is just as well because he would never have held his place in the Kent side as a batsman or bowler.

Troughton did score another hundred in his first-class career, though it wasn't for Kent. He was a member of the MCC party to the Argentine in 1911-12, captained by Lancashire's Archie MacLaren. In the match against the Combined Camps at Buenos Aires, Troughton scored 112 not out.

Troughton was a big influence on 'Tich' Freeman in his early days at Kent. He would set his field for him, discussing and explaining what he was doing. He taught Freeman a great deal, all the while using tact and firmness.

Lieutenant-Colonel Troughton's influence counted for little because Freeman wasn't included in any of the representative matches in that season.

Troughton himself may have believed that 'Tich' wasn't quite ready for this step-up, especially without his guidance. Troughton's belief would have been based on his concern for 'Tich', not through any form of arrogance.

A notable figure in Kent cricketing circles, Lionel Troughton died in 1933, still in the post as general manager of the county club. He will always be remembered as the man who was so influential in 'Tich' Freeman's early years.

Derek Underwood

Birthplace:	Bromley, Kent
Born:	8 June 1945
Died:	
Played:	1963-1987

Averages in all first-class Kent matches:

Matches	Innings	Not Outs	Runs	Highest Score	Average	100s
519	538	154	3,793	111	9.87	1

Runs	Wickets	Average	Best Analysis	5wI	10wM	Catches
37,578	1,952	19.25	9 for 28	127	38	183

Number of Test Appearances: 86

The father of Derek Underwood, himself a medium-pace bowler with the Farnborough, Kent, side, had one burning ambition – that his son should play at county level. To this end, a matting wicket was laid over concrete in their Keston garden. It wasn't long before the easy action and gentle run of Derek Underwood was born.

He attended Beckenham and Penge Grammar School, where he hit a near-hundred in a staff match. But it was his bowling which gained him ultimate recognition and a representative trial. Initially, he played with the Kent schools before progressing to the South of England Boys XI. With him in both of these representative sides was Alan Knott. Whilst playing for the South of England Boys XI, he took 4 for 6 against the Midlands at Cranleigh, but unfortunately he never went on to play for England schoolboys.

Even though he was born in Kent, Underwood watched his cricket at the Oval. He was later coached by Ken Barrington and Tony Lock, both of whom suggested that he was given a trial by Kent. He signed for Kent in 1962, making his debut the following season in May 1963. It was probably the car accident that Dave Halfyard suffered which prompted Kent to blood Underwood. His debut was against Yorkshire and his 4 for 40 secured his place for the rest of the season. It proved to be a tremendous season for him. He headed the county averages, taking 101 wickets at a cost of 21.12 runs each. He was the youngest ever to take 100 wickets in his debut season.

The following year of 1964 was another successful one. Derek had learned a lot, varying the angle by sometimes going over the wicket, turning the ball a little more and varying the pace. He once again

153

surpassed the hundred-wicket mark, taking 101 wickets at a cost of 23.52 runs each. During this season he produced his best ever bowling figures, 9 for 28 against Sussex at Hastings. He was also the second youngest to be awarded his Kent county cap.

In 1966 he headed the first-class bowling averages, the first Kent man to do so since Colin Blythe in 1914, when he took 157 wickets. In the County Championship, Underwood took 144 wickets at 12.49 runs each, his best performance being 9 for 37 against Essex at Westcliff. He was voted Best Young Cricketer of the Year and went on to make his Test debut.

His first game for his country was against the West Indies at Trent Bridge. He impressed with his bowling, but showed great determination (not for the first time) with a useful tail-enders innings. In this very match he took a nasty bouncer in the teeth from West Indian pace-man Charlie Griffith.

In 1967 he once again topped a hundred wickets, taking 128 wickets at 12.16 runs each (the best season's average of his career).

In 1968, and again in 1969, he headed the English Test Match bowling averages with outstanding figures. The most remembered of his match-winning performances for England came in 1968 at the Oval. A thunderstorm appeared to have deprived England of victory. The storm-flooded ground helped him as he destroyed the Australians with a dramatic return of 7 for 50. It was a great performance, as the wickets had to be got against time and the odds were certainly against him. Also in this series he was to show again his cool head as a batsman. At Headingley he came in at number eleven when England were 74 behind. He scored 45 not out, putting 61 on with Warwickshire's David Brown. His runs were scored not by slogging but by waiting for the right ball and then placing it sensibly.

When he toured 'Down Under' in 1970-71 it was suggested by some of the Australian press that he bowled too quickly, didn't give the ball enough air and was loathe to experiment by going over the wicket. However, he finished second in England's wicket-takers and over a quarter of the overs he bowled were maidens. When the party moved on to New Zealand, Underwood took 5 for 12 in the first innings and 6 for 85 in the second, almost winning the match single-handed! It was during this match that Underwood took his 100th Test wicket.

As well as taking wickets, he possessed great accuracy which tied down even the best of batsmen. The following season Kent played Lancashire in the Gillette Cup Final. Farokh Engineer was at the crease and attempting to hit every ball on the leg-side. His stroke was cramped due to over after over of unplayable length just outside his off-stump.

In 1973 Underwood showed his importance to the one-day game. Kent had just beaten Worcestershire in the Benson and Hedges Final at Lord's and had to travel up to Northampton for a John Player fixture the next day. Kent scored 257 and then Underwood went to work, taking 4 for 9 as Northamptonshire were bowled out for 67.

The following season, whilst playing for England in the match against Pakistan at the Oval, he took 8 for 51 on what it must be said was a difficult wicket. He had already taken 5 for 20 in the first innings, but was unplayable in the second, as the pitch covers had let rainwater through during the night. Unfortunately, his efforts went unrewarded as time ran out before England could claim victory.

In 1977 he performed the hat-trick at Hove in the match against Sussex. The following summer he took 9 wickets in an innings for the third time, when he took 9 for 32 against Surrey at the Oval. That summer he took 110 Championship wickets at a cost of 14.49 runs apiece.

In 1977 Derek Underwood decided to join the World Series Cricket. He left the Test match circuit after helping England to win the 1977 Jubilee series against Australia. When he came back, he played in only a further 12 Tests, including tours to Australia in 1979-80 and India 1981-82. He ended his international career after 86 appearances and 297 wickets.

In 1982 he was one of the cricketers banned from Test matches for three years because he had toured South Africa with an unauthorised English team. In 1983 he passed 100 wickets in a season for the seventh time, taking 106 wickets at 19.20 runs apiece.

Derek Underwood was often classed as a slow left-arm spinner, but this was technically wrong. Derek would cut the ball rather than spin it and although he possessed a clever range of pace changes, he was primarily slow-medium.

He carried his nickname 'Deadly' through his movement and pace ability to get the ball to almost stand up. Derek was a match-winner at any level, due to his accuracy and perseverance.

In 1984 against surely his most favourite of counties, Sussex, he hit his only hundred – reward for many seasons of brave and determined batting.

Derek Underwood MBE played his last game for Kent at Canterbury against Leicestershire at the end of the 1987 season. In all first-class matches he took 2,465 wickets – the 14th highest of all time. Facts and figures cannot fully portray his talents, but Derek Leslie Underwood was, without doubt, the hardest trier of all.

Bryan Valentine

Birthplace:	Blackheath, London
Born:	17 January 1908
Died:	2 February 1983
Played:	1927-1948

Averages in all first-class Kent matches:

Matches	Innings	Not Outs	Runs	Highest Score	Average	100s
308	491	28	14,131	242	30.52	25

Runs	Wickets	Average	Best Analysis	5wI	10wM	Catches
648	18	36.00	2 for 8	—	—	243

Number of Test Appearances: 7

Bryan Herbert Valentine MC was a very gifted all-round athlete. Whilst attending Repton he won the public schools lawn tennis with the well-known H W Austin. At Cambridge University he got a Blue for soccer and later became a scratch golfer.

Fortunately for lovers of cricket, and Kent cricket in particular, he devoted himself to that game.

Whilst he was at Repton, he played in the First XI for three seasons. Without doubt, 1925 was his best season, but the following year was marred by illness and injury.

In 1928 at Cambridge he made 114 (retired) in only 75 minutes in a Freshman's match. It was the following year when he was awarded his Blue. The match was against a very strong Free Foresters bowling side. Even then, his place was in doubt right up to the last minute. He certainly put everyone's mind at rest, with a super 101, scored in just 85 minutes.

He started to play for Kent in 1927, the year after he left Repton, but had only played with a moderate success. It was another four years, in 1931, before he secured a regular place in the Kent First XI line-up.

In these early days Valentine was a very promising county batsman. He was capable of playing a very entertaining and exhilerating innings with brilliant strokes, especially on the leg-side. However, in this period he was suspect in his defence.

By the mid-thirties he had become a potential Test player. He had improved his defence and learned to watch the turning ball. He had become a formidable on-driver of the many in-swing and off-spin bowlers that the new lbw law had produced. He still refused to be bogged down and scored at around 50 runs per hour. The English batting was strong and

157

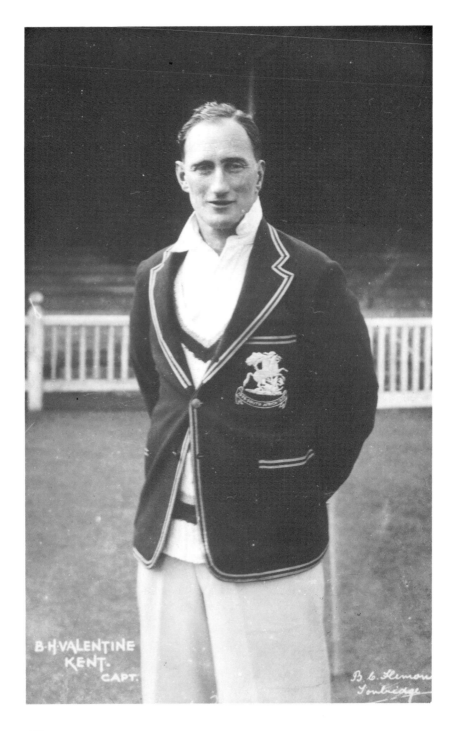

B.H.VALENTINE
KENT.
CAPT.

B. C. Hemon
Tonbridge

158

so his Test cricket was limited. In the summer of 1933 he scored 1,653 runs at an average of 36.73 and so, in the close season, was chosen to tour India with MCC. In the first Test at Bombay, Valentine scored 136 in under three hours.

In 1938 he made the highest score of his career: 242 at Oakham against Leicestershire. Altogether, he scored 1,400 first-class runs at an average of 46.66.

In 1938-39 he toured South Africa, where his consistent batting brought him an average of 45.38, including a brilliant 112 at Cape Town in the second Test. The following summer Valentine hit another double hundred: 201 against Nottinghamshire at Trent Bridge.

Perhaps it is some indication of the strength in depth of the English batting before the war that, though he averaged 64.85 in seven Tests against other countries, he never represented England against Australia. This was rather surprising because as well as being a high-scoring batsman, he was also a superb fielder.

After the war, during which he was awarded the MC and serverely wounded, he returned to captain Kent from 1946 to 1948. He shared the captaincy with Jack Bryan in 1937 and had captained the side in the absence of Percy Chapman. In 1946 in the match against Nottinghamshire at Gillingham, he hit 95 and 114 (including 9 sixes, 7 of which were in his hundred) – Kent's first post-war points.

Though as a bowler Valentine only took 18 wickets for Kent at a cost of 36 runs each, he occasionally opened the bowling when Percy Chapman was captain. Chapman's thinking behind this move (with which Valentine agreed) was that nobody would get the shine off the ball for Freeman quicker!

Valentine took his cricket seriously. He was as keen as anyone to win, but throughout he never forgot that cricket is a game. He certainly enjoyed it himself and did his utmost to ensure that others enjoyed it too. As one post-war England skipper remarked: 'What fun county cricket must have been when men like that were captain!'

In all first-class matches, he scored 18,306 runs with an average of 30.15, including 35 centuries.

He became President of Kent in 1967 and served on the Committee for many years. He never lost touch with his beloved county, constantly attending Kent matches. He died in February 1983, aged 75, a much loved and cheerful man.

Robert Wilson

Birthplace:	Bapchild, Kent
Born:	18 February 1928
Died:	
Played:	1952-1967

Averages in all first-class Kent matches:

Matches	Innings	Not Outs	Runs	Highest Score	Average	100s
365	644	38	19,458	159*	32.10	30

Runs	Wickets	Average	Best Analysis	5wI	10wM	Catches
90	4	22.50	3 for 38	—	—	200

Number of Test Appearances: 0

Bob Wilson made his Kent debut in 1952, always batting within his limitations and adapting himself to the conditions. He was a very straight batsman, yet never afraid to attack. As a left-hander, he scored runs with great consistency.

In 1954 he passed the thousand-run mark, scoring 1,433 runs in the County Championship at an average of 27.03. He was to surpass a thousand runs per season for thirteen consecutive summers. His best year was 1964, when he scored 2,038 runs at an average of 46.31.

As an attacking stroke-player, Bob Wilson was very unlucky not to have played for England. He was certainly one of the best uncapped batsmen of his time. Wilson looked good enough for a higher class of cricket – much better than some of the players who were chosen to represent their country.

In 1959 Wilson scored 1,808 runs in the County Championship at an average of 39.30. The following season in the match against Glamorgan at Blackheath he helped Arthur Phebey put on 304 for the third wicket. In 1961 he once again topped the thousand-run mark, with 1,887 runs at an average of 37.00, one of his better innings being 117 made against Surrey at Blackheath. In 1962 Kent were well beaten by Sussex in the match at Tunbridge Wells. The only batsman to offer any resistance to Sussex's attack was Bob Wilson, who scored 84 in the first innings and 61 in the second.

In 1963 he helped South African Stuart Leary put on 283 for the Kent third wicket in the match against Northamptonshire at Kettering. Wilson totalled some 1,346 runs in Championship matches that summer.

His best season was 1964, his highest score being an undefeated 159.

As a fielder Wilson was a beautiful outfield with perfect throw. He continued in 1965 and 1966 to score his 1,000 runs per season: 1,240 (average 31.79) in 1965 and 1,025 (average 27.70) in 1966.

This stalwart Kent batsman retired at the end of the 1967 season, but from a cricketing point of view this was much too soon. In first-class matches for Kent, Wilson scored 19,458 runs at an average of 32.10.

On his retirement he became the manager of the Hastings and Thanet Building Society at Sittingbourne; presently, he is serving the third of his four years on the Kent General Committee.

Frank Woolley

Birthplace:			Tonbridge, Kent			
Born:			27 May 1887			
Died:			18 October 1978			
Played:			1906-1938			

Averages in all first-class Kent matches:

Matches	Innings	Not Outs	Runs	Highest Score	Average	100s
764	1,213	67	47,868	270	41.77	122

Runs	Wickets	Average	Best Analysis	5wI	10wM	Catches
31,653	1,680	18.84	8 for 22	115	24	773

Number of Test Appearances: 64

As a small boy, Frank 'Stork' Woolley was always to be found on the Tonbridge cricket ground. One day he was watching a slow left-hander practising in the nets. When asked if he bowled, Woolley confirmed that he was of similar style and so was asked to join in. His natural ability as both batsman and bowler attracted so much attention that, in 1903, he was engaged to take part in the morning practice and then play in a match or two in the afternoon. Woolley always remained grateful to his partner in that first net practice – Colin Blythe!

The following year Woolley became a regular member of the Tonbridge ground staff which, of course, in those days was the official Kent Nursery.

Frank Woolley played in his first match for Kent at Old Trafford during June 1906. It was an unusual debut, to say the least. Lancashire batted first, scoring 531 in just five hours. J T Tyldesley scored 295 not out, being dropped twice by Woolley, whose 26 overs and one wicket cost him 103 runs. Next day, Woolley was bowled straightaway for 0. In Kent's second innings Woolley, batting at number eight, scored a pulsating 64 in an hour, cutting and pulling Lancashire's pace-man, Walter Brearley. In his third match, against Surrey at the Oval, his all-round form came as nothing less than a revelation. Surrey batted first, Woolley took the wickets of Hayes (no relation to the author!), Goatly and the great Tom Hayward. He then scored 72, top score in Kent's total of 200. In Surrey's second innings, he took 5 for 82 and then finally hit 23 not out to help Kent win an exciting game by one wicket. Also that season, he scored a hundred against Hampshire in ninety minutes at Tonbridge, his home town. It is a fact that in Woolley's first season with Kent, they won the County Championship.

In 1909 he made his Test debut, playing for England against Australia at the Oval. This was also the season that, along with Arthur Fielder, he set the Kent record for the tenth wicket, when they put on 235 against Worcestershire at Stourbridge. In 1910 he achieved the double for the first time, scoring 1,050 runs (average 25.60) and taking 132 wickets (average 13.97).

The following season, in the match against Somerset at Tunbridge Wells, he scored a century in each innings, 104 and 148 not out. During the close season tour of Australia, he hit his most spectacular pre-war innings. At Hobart, Tasmania, he scored 303 not out, including two sixes and 47 fours. In 1912 he scored 1,373 runs at an average of 45.76, also taking 107 wickets at a cost of 14.48 runs each.

As a bowler, Woolley had obviously modelled his action on Charlie Blythe, but he did bowl a little quicker and from a greater height. In 1912 at the Oval against Australia, Woolley took five wickets in each of Australia's innings. His figures being:

O	M	R	W
9.4	3	29	5
7.4	1	20	5

In 1913 he hit his first double hundred, an unbeaten 224 against Oxford University at Oxford. In 1914 he completed his third double, scoring 2,102 runs (average 47.77) and captured 119 wickets at a cost of 19.26 runs apiece. His best performance came at Gloucester when he scored 77 and 111 not out and took 12 for 122.

Frank took a very keen interest in his new bats. His particular tastes included having four heavy bats (around 2lbs 6ozs) made for him – he calculated that this number would cover his season's needs.

It was very ironic that a man of Woolley's brilliant batting ability should be turned down by the Army during the First World War because of poor eyesight!

When cricket resumed after the war in 1919, he performed the hat-trick for the only time in his career, against Surrey at Blackheath. In 1920 he scored 1,548 runs at an average of 39.69 and took 164 wickets at a cost of only 13.43 runs each. When Kent played Sussex at Horsham that season, Woolley hit 139 not out and took 10 for 132, another fine all-round performance. In 1921 he completed the cricketers double for the fifth time, scoring 1,638 (average 46.80) and taking 129 wickets (at a cost of 16.08 runs apiece). Gloucestershire were the side to suffer at Maidstone that season, as he scored 174 and took 11 for 66. However, his best remembered performance was in the Lord's Test against the Australians, when he held England together against Gregory and McDonald. Woolley scored 95 out of 187 and 93 out of 283, playing his strokes with plenty of time to spare against the powerful Aussies.

F.E. WOOLLEY
KENT.
PHOTO B.G.FLEMONS
TONBRIDGE.

164

In 1922 he achieved the sixth and last of his double seasons, scoring 1,868 runs (average 53.37) and taking 142 wickets (at a cost of 18.00 runs each). At the Oval that season, Woolley scored 100 in 101 minutes, *The Times* describing it as 'a sedate innings'.

The following season he hit the highest score of his career in this country, 270 against Middlesex at Canterbury. He was also an outstanding slip fielder in this period and took 42 catches this season. He bettered this total by two in 1935; no fieldsman, bar wicket-keepers, have approached his number of catches, which total over 1,000 in his career. Over the next couple of seasons, Woolley hit two further double centuries, 215 against Somerset at Gravesend and 217 at Northampton in 1926. The following summer, Woolley made 141 not out in 165 minutes against Middlesex at Folkestone. Jack Durston had looked unplayable as the remainder of the Kent side succumbed to the ball that flew at head height. Not so Woolley, he would cut downwards and deliberately lift the ball over the slips.

In 1928 Woolley hit his highest number of runs in a season: 2,894 at an average of 59.06. In all matches that summer in England, his runs totalled 3,352. At Folkestone this season an England XI needed 286 to beat the touring West Indies. The three West Indian fast-bowlers, Constantine, Francis and Griffiths certainly set out to intimidate the English batsmen. Woolley was unaware of any trouble and hit the bowlers to all parts of the ground. He went on to score 151 in three hours, as the England XI won by four wickets. Woolley must have been bitterly disappointed at the end of the season, after scoring so many runs, not to be selected for the winter tour of Australia.

In 1929 Woolley scored 2,040 runs (average 48.57) in the County Championship. It was the season when he hit four consecutive centuries: 155 v Derbyshire at Chesterfield; 108 v Somerset at Tonbridge; 131 v Yorkshire at Tunbridge Wells; and 117 v Hampshire at Folkestone. In 1930 at Canterbury, against the touring Australians, Woolley hit 60 in no time at all, the majority coming off Alan Fairfax who, on asking his skipper Vic Richardson if he thought it was 'all right bowling at his off stump?' was told: 'All right? It's bloody marvellous – we're all enjoying it.'

The year of 1931 was a good one for Woolley. He scored 2,011 runs at an average of 49.04. His top score that summer was 224 against New Zealand at Canterbury. It was whilst compiling that score, that he and Les Ames put on 277 for the fifth wicket to set a Kent record. Woolley also completed a hundred before lunch on two occasions; the first being against Surrey at Blackheath in 1930 and then three years later when Derbyshire were the visitors to Canterbury.

Woolley had a mixed season in 1934, scoring 2,540 runs at an average of 50.80 and, along with Bill Ashdown, helped set the Kent second wicket record, putting on 352 against Essex at Brentwood. he also had a big disappointment that summer. He was rather unwisely re-called for the fifth Test against Australia. Les Ames ricked his back and Woolley had to keep wicket in the second innings. He let through 37 byes, extras being third top scorer in the innings and England lost by 562 runs – it was a disastrous end to his Test career, and certainly one that he did not deserve.

However, in 1935 Woolley had another good year, scoring 2,339 runs (average 41.76). His top score was 229 against Surrey at the Oval in 190 minutes. Despite the years rolling on, Woolley's attitude to batting never changed. At Dover in 1937 he showed the Gloucestershire attack his particular style of playing. To win the game, Kent needed 217 to win in a little over one-and-a-half hours. Woolley opened the batting and hit 44 out of 68 in just twenty-five minutes, Kent going on to win with twenty-four minutes to spare.

On his retirement in 1938, it was fitting that he should captain the Players in their match against the Gentlemen at Lord's.

Woolley played first-class cricket from 1906 to 1938, from his nineteenth to his fifty-first year. In his career, he scored 58,969 runs at an average of 40.75, with 145 hundreds. He certainly didn't enjoy getting out. He would frequently stand at the crease for a few split-seconds after an appeal had been granted against him!

Standing at six feet three inches, Woolley fully justified the soubriquet 'Stalky'. Because of his tallness and his reach, he could make strokes in a wide range without obvious adjustments of feet and body. Certainly no batsman has hit the ball harder or further for a longer period of time than Frank Woolley.

After his retirement from the game, he was elected a life member of the MCC and Kent and also the county committee. In the 1950s he worked at Butlin's Holiday Camp, Clacton, coaching guests and organising net practice. He was quite active into his late 80s and in January 1971 he flew to Australia to watch the last two Tests. Nine months later, in Canada, he married for the second time, his first wife having died some ten years earlier.

Frank Woolley died in Halifax, Nova Scotia, on 18 October 1978 at the age of 91, one of the finest and most elegant of left-handed all-rounders in the history of the game.

Bob Woolmer

Birthplace:	Kanpur, India	
Born:	14 May 1948	
Died:		
Played:	1968-1984	

Averages in all first-class Kent matches:

Matches	Innings	Not Outs	Runs	Highest Score	Average	100s
279	428	68	12,634	203	35.09	28

Runs	Wickets	Average	Best Analysis	5wI	10wM	Catches
7,810	334	23.38	7 for 47	12	1	195 (plus 1 st)

Number of Test Appearances: 19

Robert Andrew Woolmer was born in Kanpur, India, not far from the cricket ground. He was the son of a British business executive who had captained Uttar Pradesh at cricket. He lived in India until he was 7 years old, but then moved to England to begin his cricketing education at Yardley Court, Tonbridge. At Yardley Court he was under the guidance of A F Brickmore, a former Kent player, who was headmaster of the school. He later moved on to Skinners School, Tonbridge, where at the age of 15 he came to the notice of the Kent Second XI captain and coach, Colin Page. It was Page who suggested to Woolmer that he would be more effective as a medium-pace bowler than an off-spinner.

Woolmer took up a post as sales representative with ICI in London, but during his holidays he played with Tunbridge Wells. It wasn't long before he found himself asked to play for the Kent Second XI.

At the age of 20, in 1968, he joined the Kent ground staff. Page wanted him to settle in and warned him that it could be a couple of years before he was even considered for first-team duty. However, he was needed sooner than expected and he made his debut in the Maidstone week against Essex. He wasn't asked to bowl, but did make an unbeaten half-century. In fact, he ran out Stuart Leary and was about to give his wicket up when umpire Cec Pepper overruled him and called him back. Woolmer had a few more matches that summer and began to develop his bowling.

In 1969 he took 7 for 47 against Sussex at Canterbury and 4 for 12 against Middlesex at Lord's, both in the County Championship. In the John Player League, he impressed greatly, taking wickets for Kent with his ability to move the ball about at medium-pace.

In 1970 he was awarded his county cap, and at the end of that season he spent the winter coaching in South Africa. It was here that after hours of

practice, he perfected his bowling armoury by learning to swing the ball away. In 1972 he picked up 13 wickets in the match with Sussex (6 for 70 and 7 for 65).

Two years later, Woolmer began to string some good scores together. He hit hundreds against Derbyshire, Somerset and Sussex in the Championship. In 1975 he performed the hat-trick for the MCC against the Australians at Lord's and later made his Test debut on the same ground. He was left out after his debut until the last match of the series at the Oval. He scored 149; it was the slowest hundred ever made by an England batsman against Australia. It took him 6 hours 34 minutes against the previous slowest, 6 hours 2 minutes by another Kent cricketing great, Colin Cowdrey. Oh for a century like that in last year's Test series for the Ashes!

In 1976 he began to open the batting for Kent, passing the thousand-run mark in Championship cricket for the first time. He scored 1,461 runs at an average of 56.19, also taking over 50 wickets. He also took five catches in an innings against Worcestershire to show his all-round talent.

At Test level, he was perhaps regarded as a batsman who could bowl rather than a genuine all-rounder.

In 1977 he scored centuries against Australia at Lord's and Old Trafford. Including the Centenary Test, he had made seven appearances against the old enemy, scoring three hundreds. It equalled Peter May's record and was better than Grace, Graveney or Woolley. For Kent he was also in fine form. Despite missing eight matches he finished top of the county's first-class batting averages.

After 15 appearances for his country, he joined the World Series Cricket founded by Kerry Packer. His gain financially was lost in the momentum of his Test career. He did play in four further games for England in 1980 and 1981, but couldn't reach his original heights. In his nineteen Tests, Woolmer scored 1,059 runs at an average of 33.09.

In 1978 and 1979 he once again topped the thousand-run mark, scoring 1,245 runs (average 40.16) in 1978 and 1,382 runs (average 40.64) in 1979.

In 1982 he hit the highest score of his career, 203 against Sussex at Tunbridge Wells.

He played his last game for Kent in 1984; a graceful right-handed batsman and useful medium-fast bowler, who always remained loyal to the county that gave him his chance.

Doug Wright

Birthplace:	Sidcup, Kent
Born:	21 August 1914
Died:	
Played:	1932-1957

Averages in all first-class Kent matches:

Matches	Innings	Not Outs	Runs	Highest Score	Average	100s
397	595	188	5,074	84*	12.46	—

Runs	Wickets	Average	Best Analysis	5wI	10wM	Catches
38,774	1,709	22.68	9 for 47	132	38	152

Number of Test Appearances: 34

Douglas Vivian Parson Wright was born in Sidcup in 1914. In his early days he was thought of as a promising batsman, but he didn't develop in this respect. This was probably due to the fact that he was trying to work at his action. He bowled with a bounding run, often compared with a kangaroo's hopping. He spun the ball hard which not all English leg-spinner did.

Wright's action was certainly odd, often prone to bowling no-balls. He first played for Kent in 1932, though his real chance came when 'Tich' Freeman retired from the Kent side at the end of the 1936 season. As a leg-spinner he was faster than most of his kind, not like the man he replaced, Freeman. He possessed a very fast ball which took many wickets, and a googly that colleagues would have liked to have seen more often!

During each of the next five seasons, excluding the war years, Wright took 100 wickets or more. In 1948 he chipped a finger and was restricted to claiming only 77 victims! Yet the following year, fully recovered, he once again passed the hundred mark.

In 1937 he took 111 wickets at a cost of 27.19 each, including two hat-tricks at Worcester and Trent Bridge.

Wright made his Test debut in 1938 against the touring Australians. His appearance was, in the main, due to his good-performance in a Test trial. In his younger days he was often spoken of as a kind of bowler who 'will win a Test match one day'. This he never did, but throughout his international career he was the bowler most likely to capture a wicket at any time, and in any conditions. At the end of that season, Australian captain Bradman said that he would have liked to have had Wright in his side.

In 1938-39 he toured South Africa, taking yet another hat-trick at East London in the match against Border. The season at home saw Wright take 131 wickets at a cost of 15.65 runs each. His best match figures that summer were 16 for 80 against Somerset at Bath. His best match analysis came in the match against Gloucestershire at Bristol, when he took 9 for 47, including the hat-trick.

In 1946 Wright resumed where he'd left off some seven years earlier, taking 113 wickets at 17.63 runs each. When he toured Australia in 1946-47, there wasn't one single Australian batsman who could master Wright's bowling. Unfortunately, there were a great number of missed chances, the majority off his bowling.

This is highlighted by the fifth Test at Sydney. In the last innings, Australia need 214 to win. At 45 for 1, in marched the great Bradman. He'd only made 2, when he snicked a superb leg-break from Wright, straight into and then through first-slip's hands. Australia went on to win the match and the series, but who knows what might have happened if that chance had been held. In that match, Wright took 7 for 105 and 2 for 93. He toured Australia twice and South Africa twice, playing in 34 Tests in all, taking 108 wickets at 39.11.

It was the second half of the 1947 season that Wright struck superb form. He altered his field somewhat; instead of an attack aimed generally at the middle and off, he substituted one intended for the leg or the middle and leg with three close fielders on the leg side. The runs off the edge dried up and those batsmen that didn't spot the googly and pushed out at the delivery were more often than not caught at short-leg.

In 1947 Wright took 142 wickets at 19.01 each. His best performance that season was 15 for 173 against Sussex at Hastings, including the fifth hat-trick of his career. Two years later, he had 128 wickets at 21.21 each, his best match performance being against Leicestershire at Maidstone, when he took 15 for 163. In the first innings of that match he took 9 for 51. Also that season, in the match against Hampshire at Canterbury, he took the seventh hat-trick of his career. This achievement is presently the world record.

In 1950 he took 141 wickets to gain him his place on the 1950-51 tour of Australia and New Zealand. Though he was rather expensive in the Australian Tests, he was instrumental in England gaining their first post-war victory over the Aussies. Then, in New Zealand, he took 5 for 48 in what turned out to be the last of his 34 Test matches.

Wright was also more than a useful batsman, good enough to average around 20 in his best seasons. He was also a very competent fielder, once taking six catches in an innings. He was also the first officially appointed professional Captain of Kent, captaining the team from 1954 to 1956.

If Doug Wright had played his cricket under a shrewd tactician and the war hadn't taken away his best years, I'm sure he would have been hailed as one of the greatest English spin bowlers of all time.

After retiring from first-class cricket, he became professional and coach at Charterhouse.

In all first-class matches, Wright took 2,056 wickets at an average of 23.98. They are very impressive figures, yet some in Kent thought he didn't do his talents justice. Yet, for the author, he was the last of the great English leg-spinners.

Appendices

Statistical Analysis

Whilst it is purely a matter of opinion as to how good a player a man is, or has been, and it is certainly true that figures seldom tell the true story of any cricketer, the author hopes the following will go some way to explaining why he has chosen the following eleven players as his team of 'Kent Great':

1. Les Ames
2. Arthur Fagg
3. Colin Cowdrey
4. Wally Hardinge
5. Jack Mason (Captain)
6. Frank Woolley
7. Alan Knott
8. Arthur Fielder
9. Colin Blythe
10. Derek Underwood
11. 'Tich' Freeman

Kent Top Tens

The following section lists the best performances in each of several categories, showing in statistical form the 'top ten' for Kent:

MOST MATCHES

1.	F E Woolley	764
2.	H T W Hardinge	606
3.	J Seymour	536
4.	D L Underwood	519
5.	A P Freeman	506
6.	W H Ashdown	482
7.	F H Huish	469
8.	L E G Ames	430
9.	L J Todd	426
10.	A E Fagg	414

MOST WICKETS

1.	A P Freeman	3,340
2.	C Blythe	2,210
3.	D L Underwood	1,952
4.	D V P Wright	1,709
5.	F E Woolley	1,680
6.	A Fielder	1,150
7.	A Hearne	1,018
8.	F Ridgway	955
9.	A L Dixon	929
10.	W J Fairservice	853

MOST RUNS

1.	F E Woolley	47,868
2.	H T W Hardinge	32,549
3.	L E G Ames	29,851
4.	J Seymour	26,818
5.	A E Fagg	26,072
6.	M C Cowdrey	23,779
7.	W H Ashdown	22,309
8.	R C Wilson	19,458
9.	L J Todd	19,407
10.	B W Luckhurst	19,096

MOST TEST APPEARANCES

1.	M C Cowdrey	114
2.	A P E Knott	95
3.	T G Evans	91
4.	D L Underwood	86
5.	F E Woolley	64
6.	Asif Iqbal	58
7.	L E G Ames	47
8.	D V P Wright	34
9.	C J Tavare	30
10.	M H Denness	28

MOST HUNDREDS

1.	F E Woolley	122
2.	L E G Ames	78
3.	H T W Hardinge	73
4.	M C Cowdrey	58
5.	A E Fagg	55
6.	J Seymour	53
7.	B W Luckhurst	39
8.	W H Ashdown	38
9.	L J Todd	36
10.=	M R Benson	31
	J R Mason	31

MOST CATCHES (Fieldsmen)

1.	F E Woolley	773
2.	J Seymour	659
3.	A E Fagg	411
4.	M C Cowdrey	406
5.	W H Ashdown	398
6.	S E Leary	362
7.	J R Mason	360
8.	A Hearne	352
9.	B W Luckhurst	350
10.	M H Denness	308

BATTING AVERAGES

1. L E G Ames   44.33
2. M R Benson*   42.11
3. M C Cowdrey   42.01
4. F E Woolley   41.77
5. C J Burnup   38.06
6. B W Luckhurst   38.00
7. C J Tavare   37.97
8. Asif Iqbal   37.06
9. H T W Hardinge   36.48
10. A E Fagg   36.06

* Still playing first-class cricket.

BOWLING AVERAGES

1. D W Carr   15.61
2. G G Hearne   16.50
3. C Blythe   16.67
4. A P Freeman   17.64
5. F E Woolley   18.84
6. D L Underwood   19.25
7. A Hearne   19.96
8. C S Marriott   20.28
9. A Fielder   20.88
10. J R Mason   22.06

There are other players with better bowling averages, but they haven't been included as they haven't played enough matches to warrant inclusion as a Kent Cricketing Great.

HIGHEST SCORES

1.	W H Ashdown	332	v	Essex	1934
2.	L E G Ames	295	v	Gloucestershire	1933
3.	F E Woolley	270	v	Middlesex	1923
4.	A E Fagg	269*	v	Nottinghamshire	1953
5.	H T W Hardinge	263*	v	Gloucestershire	1928
6.	A P F Chapman	260	v	Lancashire	1927
7.	M C Cowdrey	250	v	Essex	1959
8.	B H Valentine	242	v	Leicestershire	1938
9.	J Seymour	218*	v	Essex	1911
10.	B W Luckhurst	215	v	Derbyshire	1973

Also scored:

W H Ashdown	305*	v	Derbyshire	1935
F E Woolley	229	v	Surrey	1935
F E Woolley	224	v	Oxford University	1913
F E Woolley	224	v	New Zealand	1931
A E Fagg	257	v	Hampshire	1936
A E Fagg	244	v	Essex	1938
A E Fagg	221	v	Nottinghamshire	1951
H T W Hardinge	249*	v	Leicestershire	1922
†J L Bryan	236	v	Hampshire	1923
†D G Aslett	221*	v	Sri Lanka	1984

†Would normally figure in the list, but neither have been classed as a Kent Cricketing Great.

Kent Cricketing Greats
Batting Averages

(Up to the end of the 1989 season)

	Matches	Innings	Not Outs	Runs	H. Sc.	Average
L E G Ames	430	717	64	29,851	295	44.33
W H Ashdown	482	804	76	22,309	332	30.64
M R Benson	189	311	26	12,002	162	42.11
C Blythe	381	506	111	3,964	82*	10.03
W M Bradley	123	185	50	795	67*	5.88
C J Burnup	157	271	17	9,668	200	38.06
D W Carr	49	54	13	398	48	9.70
F G H Chalk	101	169	12	4,436	198	28.25
A P F Chapman	194	269	21	6,681	260	26.93
G C Collins	212	316	37	6,237	110	22.35
M C Cowdrey	402	651	85	23,779	250	42.01
M H Denness	333	562	44	17,047	178	32.90
G R Dilley	109	116	39	993	81	12.89
E W Dillon	223	348	22	9,415	141	28.88
A L Dixon	378	576	71	9,561	125*	18.93
P R Downton	45	45	10	396	31	11.31
A G E Ealham	305	466	68	10,996	153	27.62
T G Evans	258	451	15	9,325	144	21.38
A E Fagg	414	767	44	26,072	269*	36.06
W J Fairservice	301	417	96	4,922	61*	15.33
A Fielder	253	329	154	2,000	112*	11.42
A P Freeman	506	630	170	4,257	66	9.25
D J Halfyard	185	274	31	2,538	79	10.44
H T W Hardinge	606	990	98	32,549	263*	36.48
Lord Harris	157	278	17	7,842	176	30.04
A. Hearne	403	687	63	13,598	162*	21.79
G G Hearne	252	444	44	7,148	126	17.87
J C Hubble	343	496	61	10,229	189	23.51
F H Huish	469	686	122	7,247	93	12.84
E Humphreys	366	590	44	15,308	208	28.03
K L Hutchings	163	238	12	7,977	176	35.29
Asif Iqbal	243	399	42	13,231	171	37.06
G W Johnson	376	582	73	12,549	168	24.65
A P E Knott	349	505	94	11,339	144	27.58
W H V Levett	142	214	44	2,054	76	12.08
S E Leary	381	617	92	16,169	158	30.79
B W Luckhurst	335	568	65	19,096	215	38.00

	Matches	Innings	Not Outs	Runs	H. Sc.	Average
C S Marriott	101	105	31	356	21	4.81
J R Mason	300	491	33	15,563	183	33.98
A H Phebey	320	585	33	14,299	157	25.90
F Ridgway	298	442	100	3,812	94	11.14
J Seymour	536	881	60	26,818	218*	32.62
J N Shepherd	303	431	74	9,401	170	26.33
C J Tavare	259	425	51	14,201	168*	37.97
C I Thornton	18	34	1	959	124	29.06
L J Todd	426	709	93	19,407	174	31.50
L H W Troughton	164	235	30	3,477	104	16.96
D L Underwood	519	538	154	3,793	111	9.87
B H Valentine	308	491	28	14,131	242	30.52
R C Wilson	365	644	38	19,458	159*	32.10
F E Woolley	764	1,213	67	47,868	270	41.77
R A Woolmer	279	428	68	12,634	203	35.09
D V P Wright	397	595	188	5,074	84*	12.46

Kent Cricketing Greats
Bowling Averages
(Up to the end of the 1989 season)

	Runs	Wickets	Best	Average	Catches
L E G Ames	697	22	3-23	31.68	
W H Ashdown	19,290	595	6-23	32.42	398
M R Benson	378	3	2-55	126.00	91
C Blythe	36,859	2,210	10-30	16.67	183
W M Bradley	11,886	536	9-87	22.17	71
C J Burnup	1,795	41	5-44	43.78	74
D W Carr	4,529	290	8-36	15.61	18
F G H Chalk	137	2	2-25	68.50	40
A P F Chapman	151	3	2-24	50.33	173
G C Collins	8,964	378	10-65	23.71	79
M C Cowdrey	1,285	27	4-22	47.59	406
M H Denness	55	2	1-7	27.50	308
G R Dilley	7,146	257	6-57	27.80	51
E W Dillon	1,321	27	3-20	48.92	195
A L Dixon	23,869	929	8-61	25.69	155
P R Downton					
A G E Ealham	189	3	1-1	63.00	175
T G Evans	215	2	2-50	107.50	
A E Fagg	47	0			411
W J Fairservice	19,272	853	7-44	22.59	164
A Fielder	24,014	1,150	9-108	20.88	106
A P Freeman	58,944	3,340	10-53	17.64	202
D J Halfyard	18,822	769	9-39	24.47	88
H T W Hardinge	9,773	370	7-64	26.41	286
Lord Harris	1,523	64	5-57	23.79	155
A. Hearne	23,023	1,018	8-15	19.96	352
G G Hearne	9,393	569	8-21	16.50	175
J C Hubble	1	0			
F H Huish	87	0			
E Humphreys	8,122	306	7-33	26.54	212
K L Hutchings	493	15	4-73	32.86	141
Asif Iqbal	2,096	73	4-11	28.71	168
G W Johnson	17,058	555	7-76	30.73	271
A P E Knott	13	1	1-5	13.00	
W H V Levett	6	0			
S E Leary	4,714	140	5-22	33.67	362
B W Luckhurst	2,617	61	4-32	42.90	350

179

	Runs	Wickets	Best	Average	Catches
C S Marriott	9,391	463	7-52	20.28	26
J R Mason	16,969	769	8-29	22.06	360
A H Phebey	4	0			202
F Ridgway	22,740	955	8-39	23.81	203
J Seymour	680	15	4-62	45.33	659
J N Shepherd	22,106	832	8-83	26.56	212
C J Tavare	493	5	1-20	98.60	269
C I Thornton	205	8	2-12	25.62	12
L J Todd	15,197	555	6-26	27.38	226
L H W Troughton	20	0			72
D L Underwood	37,578	1,952	9-28	19.25	183
B H Valentine	648	18	2-8	36.00	243
R C Wilson	90	4	3-38	22.50	200
F E Woolley	31,653	1,680	8-22	18.84	773
R A Woolmer	7,810	334	7-47	23.38	195
D V P Wright	38,774	1,709	9-47	22.68	152

Wicket-Keeping

	Matches	Caught	Stumped	Total	Average no. of victims per match
F H Huish	469	901	352	1,253	2.67
L E G Ames	430*	512	330	842	1.95
A P E Knott	349	746	85	831	2.38
J C Hubble	343	411	217	628	1.83
T G Evans	258	451	103	554	2.14
W H V Levett	142	228	169	397	2.79
P R Downton	45	97	2	99	2.20

*Many matches as a pure batsman.

The author wishes to thank Mr Chris Taylor (Kent County Cricket Club Curator) for his help in compiling these statistics.